ANGELS

Guides and Goosebumps

Global Publishing Group

Australia • New Zealand • Singapore • America • London

ANGELS
Guides and Goosebumps

Spiritual Stories About Manifesting the Life You Truly Want

Linet Amaile

Julia Anais

Sonia Crystella

Leila Dal-Zotto

Karen Wilson

Steve Coleman

Selena Seah

Wanda Shipton

KAWENA (Gwen Gordon)

DISCLAIMER

All the information, techniques, skills and concepts contained within this publication are of the nature of general comment only and are not in any way recommended as individual advice. The intent is to offer a variety of information to provide a wider range of choices now and in the future, recognising that we all have widely diverse circumstances and viewpoints. Should any reader choose to make use of the information contained herein, this is their decision, and the contributors (and their companies), authors and publishers do not assume any responsibilities whatsoever under any condition or circumstances. It is recommended that the reader obtain their own independent advice.

First Edition 2017

A catalogue record for this book is available from the National Library of Australia

Published by Global Publishing Group
PO Box 517 Mt Evelyn, Victoria 3796 Australia
Email info@GlobalPublishingGroup.com.au

For further information about orders:
Phone: +61 3 9739 4686 or Fax +61 3 8648 6871

This book is dedicated to those who trusted and encouraged me on my Earthly journey.

Acknowledgements

Elizabeth Joy: My daughter Elizabeth Joy, for all your help, support, patience and creative ideas over all the years. Elizabeth is a psychic medium and author in her own right.

www.elizabethjoy.com.au

Sonia Crystella: For giving up so much of your precious time, for your expertise in helping to guide me through the book, and your patience with the editing and working with me to have it done in a manner that is different, it was very special!

www.soniacrystella.com

Tracey Stranger: Thank you for your help before the book idea originated, and for the videos on YouTube, that will help me with the personal mentoring section of the book.

www.essentialhealth.com.au

Tricia Torado: Thank you for your encouragement from the very beginning when the book idea started to grow, your encouragement was just what I needed.

www.alittleblissevents.com.au

Karin Kolenko: For your constant support along the way, and for helping me clear my head from the huge workload I had, you kept me grounded.

www.goldcoastbenji.com.au

Crystina Maxwell: Thank you for helping me to stay on track, and for being a good listener. Spiritual advisor and meditations.

mcrystina@yahoo.com.au

Darren J. Stephens and Jackie Stephens: Along with your amazing team at Global Publishing for bringing the book to fruition and for your guidance - your input was greatly appreciated.

www.globalpublishinggroup.com.au

Contents

Foreword

The book you're holding in your hands at this moment contains some of the most powerful teachings available to you on our planet today.

I've been profoundly touched and influenced by Kawena's message here in this book and deeply honoured that Kawena has asked me to provide a Foreword.

As an international bestselling author and consultant myself, I've had the privilege to consult and work with tens of thousands of people, from presidents, movie stars and Fortune 500 executives to everyday people from all walks of life, in over 27 countries.

I continually strive to help people become more successful and make a difference in the world. As someone who has travelled the world multiple times over I've witnessed first-hand many things that are hard to explain, but there's one thing I can tell you for sure… that we are all connected on a much higher level of being than you might think possible, and when you learn to embrace that spiritual/universal energy, then your world will truly change for the better.

We live in the age of information – the most fast-paced era of known history, with the super-highway known as the 'internet' where, with the touch of your computer keyboard or smartphone, you can make contact, and access information and people virtually anywhere in the world instantly. We have more choices and opportunities today than at any other time in human history. However we also have more confusion, information overload and less guidance on how to make those choices that can propel us to wealth, success and abundance.

This book is unique because you'll be fortunate to tap into the thinking of Kawena's 89 years of wisdom and of someone who is permanently connected to universal energy, angels and spirits. These voices of spirits speak in a language you'll understand and be able to instantly translate into action. They offer you no less than the blueprint for understanding and implementing your own destiny.

Allow the energy that it contains to permeate through any resistance that your body/mind might offer and let it resonate with the inner place, your unconscious mind that is deep with in all of us, this is what is often called your soul.

So it is with great pleasure that I invite you to now read Kawena's book to rediscover your true passion, to get clear about what you really want in life and to give you strategies to visualise and tap into new ways of focusing your mind, so you're able to create the extraordinary life you truly desire and deserve.

Darren J Stephens

#1 International Bestselling Author & Speaker
www.DarrenJStephens.com

Introduction

Right across the planet and for as long as the historians have kept records, and probably well before that time, people from all walks of life have talked about their visitations and apparitions from The Angels, The Guides, The Spiritual Beings, The Saints and loved ones who have passed over.

Many people will brush it aside as a hallucination or a figment of the imagination, mostly out of fear; that maybe another dimension really does exist, and that we do have the ability to tap into it. As many more of you are finding yourselves in the presence of these Beings, you are eager to learn and tune into these energies that bring about feelings of pure LOVE, messages and guidance. Alternately, objects, smells, as well as repeated numbers are turning up in your life. You might also dream of these Beings or have warning messages that can change the course of your life.

What are Angels and where do they come from? And why do we think they have wings?

What would you do if Angels appeared before you and they looked nothing at all like the pictures you see in books or the preconceived images that you have in your mind about their appearance?

But; somehow, you knew that they are indeed Angels; and that their messages and their visits will change your life, and how you view your life, 'forever'.

Kawena's first visitation from an Angel completely amazed her. The Angels different appearance, and the way that she felt in its presence along with the sensations through her body, combined with the sound of its voice, triggered the Goosebumps.

As we start to understand that we are not alone and that we have help and guidance we start to attract more of these energies and more coincidences into our life.

ANGELS

REPRESENT

KINDNESS

COURAGE

AND

LOVE

YES

I DO TALK TO ANGELS

AND YES

I HAVE VISIONED MY
THREE PERSONAL ANGELS

AND YES

I ALSO WORK WITH
THREE SPECIAL ARCHANGELS

- MICHAEL
- RAPHAEL
- GABRIEL

Michael – For planetary healing

Raphael – For personal healing and meditating

Gabriel – For writing and speaking

SECTION 1

Kawena's Story

Goosebumps

If you are wondering about the Goosebumps; I once asked Angel ALIEL why that happens to us.

Angels usually answer with one, two or three words, or sometimes a whole sentence, but this time it was quite informative.

Apparently, those feelings that we get in our bodies of icy cold prickles on various occasions is the

'Universe's Way of Saying'
YES
IT'S A GOOD THING.

You will probably remember getting them when something wonderful is happening; e.g., you've received good news – you have seen something beautiful or even heard beautiful music.

I often get them when Angels are close; you might get them when a medium brings you a special message from a loved one who has passed over.

Welcome to my World of Angel Experiences

This book has nothing to do with the theory of the Angelic realm or religion. Some people have their religious beliefs and some have their rituals, I fully respect everybody's right as to how they choose their journey.

This book is simply a sharing of my personal experiences with Angels; and how they communicate with me. My beliefs are very simple; maybe too simple for some, but in the simplicity of my connection to Angels it works perfectly, and I am very happy with that.

Your experiences with the Angelic energy may differ from mine, but it will help some of you realise that you aren't the only ones seeing and hearing things differently to others.

Knowing that, it is ok to trust your gut feelings and clairsentience (clear sensing) and also your creative thoughts.

We are fast coming to realise that it is ok to THINK – FEEL – and LOOK at life differently to others and to also know that no two people ever think the same regarding most subjects. I do like to think that there is a common thread with most of our beliefs and what suits us and that is;

THE SHARING – THE CARING and THE LOVING
WE ARE EACH A UNIQUE
ONE OF CREATION

In the Beginning

In the beginning I was guided by my Angels; to include others Angel experiences as well as my own in this book, I sensed it was necessary to choose people with **who have** different experiences, so **that** others might value and feel comfortable with their own happenings, especially when they are very different.

It is so comforting to see some cynics change their view and accept the Spiritual journey, as many young psychics have **now** stepped forward and are sharing their special gifts with the world.

Take your time, read through the book and you might be surprised at what resonates with you. As far as the Angel energy goes I am constantly amazed at how differently they present themselves to others.

It is true that there is an incredible resurgence of Angel awareness and I am hoping that mine and other author's books will help the general public, and even the cynics, accept their presence into daily conversations, thus helping to bring more peace into the world. Since writing this book – even before it was published and sold – so many are sharing their unusual experiences and miraculous happenings with me, saying that they had never felt comfortable talking about them before; but they now find it such a relief to **talk about** and **share** their experiences. I call this

'DIVINE TIMING'

Having been around for many years I have watched the Spiritual understanding grow and become accepted right across the planet. We are coming to understand that this journey is simply about

'Love and Kindness'

In my very early days, the word LOVE wasn't used much and even GOD was only mentioned on Sunday's at church; and at dinner time when we said Grace.

Public hugging and showing of affection was frowned upon, and even one generation before that had to have a chaperone (someone older than them if they went out together).

These days we seem to have gone from one extreme to the other.

ONCE YOU CONSCIOUSLY

BECOME YOUR OWN

CO-CREATOR

And

- Tune into the creative universe
- Connect with your higher self
- Accept yourself faults and all

ONCE THIS HAPPENS

NO ONE

Not one person

Can wipe the SMILE off your face

Once the connection is made.

YOU SET YOUR SPIRIT FREE!

Then you are able to cope with *absolutely* everything that life has to offer.

CHAPTER 1

The Awakening

For many years I have resisted writing a book about my Angel experiences. It has been such a relief to be able to open up after all this time and tell my story to the world; I once thought it was too simple to be believable, and besides that the Angels didn't encourage me too. *That is*; until I spoke about it to a few likeminded people, and I quickly realised that they also had had very similar experiences. For the first time I have been prompted to put pen to paper and write about my...

FUNNY

SERIOUS

HAPPY

JOYOUS

And

Unusual experiences during my lifetime with the Angels.

It is nothing like the serious theory of Angels

But it is my story

And it works for me.

I do feel I have now been guided by my Angels to write about them because of

THE HUGE SURGE of Angel energy
COMING IN TO HELP BRING
MORE PEACE TO MOTHER EARTH
AND HER INHABITANTS

I am focusing more on helping the many who want to improve their way of life and to become the best that they can possibly be.

At this stage of evolution the world needs more healers and more guidance which will help to bring a positive balance to all the negative energies out there.

It was not in my plans years ago to be doing this type of work; my life changes have amazed me more than I could imagine.

It has truly only come about with my Angels' help and encouragement that I still have the inner strength and confidence to keep up the pace, and loving every step of the journey. I am completely delighted that so many people that I have mentored are now putting themselves out there. Many of them lacked self-confidence and joy in their lives when they first came to me.

Most of us who embrace the Spiritual journey look back at the earlier parts of our lives and the tough times that we encountered, knowing now that they have led us to self-realisation and understanding.

I first became aware of the Angel energy when I was middle-aged. Before that I had never focused upon them. I had only given thought to them on various occasions.

Then once I did become more aware and invited them into my personal space, life changed and they brought so many magical sensations and achievements into my presence.

THEN EVERYTHING CHANGED WITHIN AND AROUND ME

The first change I noticed in becoming aware of their presence was that my mind opened up to incredible creative messages and learning.

It was as if I now had *company* and *support* in all my endeavours.

I now had new friends in my life, and my meditations became more in-depth and enjoyable.

For the last 39 years I have seen and heard Spiritual information slowly filtering through; now it is reaching a crescendo point which tells us we are not on a 'Human Journey' but a 'Soul Journey' – recognising this gives us creative power over our lives.

I can only think of the soul as coming from our enthusiasm, passion and energy levels, the part of us that looks for the truth – the positive – the loving and exciting part of ourselves and others.

If you think about it, it makes sense, as we realise that the word enthusiasm comes from the Greek word *ENTHEOS* which means

In GOD

The human mind will very often tell us that we can't follow our dreams,

SPIRIT ENTHUSIASTICALLY SAYS "LET'S GO!"

With this new surge of Spiritual and planetary energy we are fast becoming eager to learn more about our soul's journey and this whole 'new' concept of who and what we are.

It appears to me that the information we crave is finally being unleashed, and the understanding and excitement is now building up.

It is gratifying to see that many in higher positions within governments, religious and the business world are tapping into this **'NEW WAVE OF UNDERSTANDING'**.

They are now sharing more than ever before:

"We are all part of each other!"

I don't know about you, but ever since 2014 began, I have felt a whole new positive energy surging through humanity and across MOTHER EARTH.

We know that some negative energies will always be there to challenge us, but I feel that love and caring is about to help balance these Yin and Yang energies.

The majority of us on the Spiritual journey are peaceful people who are now feeling the need to speak up in a diplomatic and honest way. The more we spread our "LOVE AND LIGHT" across the planet the more we help ourselves, Mother Earth and Humanity.

It is so good to know that we are not alone
and
THE ANGELS and THE GUIDES
are always there
to help us.

Around the age of 40 years old I was in an incredibly bad space. I had lost so much of value in myself and my life. I had no friends and I had no help from anyone. Those days there was not the information or the help that there is now.

All I had was my positive thinking books, which had helped me through extremely hard times. There was a point where I was at the desperate stage and didn't know where to turn, so I tried to leave the planet…

"BUT I DIDN'T QUITE MAKE IT."

I had no idea about Angel energies or the Spiritual journey; I was just an everyday housewife and mother and not even highly educated. Looking back I remember very little about that time in my life, but the one thing that has stayed with me is the feeling of being out of my body and in that peaceful vacuum of nothingness.

Of course I know now that the Angels were at work as it;

"WASN'T MY TIME."

Once I surfaced from the deep depression I realised that I was creating my own unhappiness by complaining constantly to myself about everything that was going wrong in my life, and I remembered reading what Norman Vincent Peale had written in his book called *The Power of Positive Thinking.*

> *"We manufacture our own unhappiness by practicing negative thinking and we manufacture our own happiness by positive thinking."*

His book is just as powerful now as it was then and **it** will never go out of date.

Looking Back

It is not much fun when we are young and are going through really tough times; but as we get older our main aim seems to be to look for the good that came out of it.

When I look back; I am surprised how much good did come out of those negative experiences I endured, especially when I started to understand why they happened. I now know that UNIVERSE often brings us a far better dream than we could have imagined:

IT DID FOR ME!

It is also true that when we are young most of us don't understand, value, or even appreciate what we had

'UNTIL WE LOST IT.'

I was never really aware of being grateful for what I had. I just took it all for granted; especially when something good came into my life – I just assumed I was lucky.

On looking back (as we do) I can see how each failure, disappointment and even the successes led me to where

I am now and the work that I do. My present day life was never in my plan for my future; even becoming an author was way out of my reach, and as for now being called the Gold Coast Spiritual Matriarch, back then I would have laughed till I cried.

I still have life's lessons; but my attitude and understanding is very different now.

We come to learn that the harder the road, the more empathy and understanding we have of others and their challenges; this helps us to be the best guides and mentors of the present, and of the future.

We used to revere the elderly and call them the wise ones; I feel that many of my readers will understand this chapter more than any other.

My full understanding of life did not start until I was around 50 years old when I decided to learn to sing. It was then that I learned the strength of the power of the breath and the positive effect it has on us. From that very moment I have never looked back, it has been a magical rollercoaster ride.

Personal Notes

CHAPTER 2

Seeing and Hearing Their Words for the First Time

Many years ago my daughter Elizabeth returned home from our local shopping centre and said, "Mum I have found a pack of Angel cards with a book, by Ambika Wauters and you might be interested in them." Without hesitation I knew I had to return to the shop and buy them, I was fast becoming very conscious of the Angel energy.

The first visitation came one night while I was watching TV; it was then that I noticed movement out the peripheral vision of my left eye. Turning to look and see what it was, I saw sitting on the lounge an old Chinese gentleman, dressed in a stunning green and gold brocade jacket. He was almost bald, except for a long thick plait curving around his shoulder. It was at this point that our eyes *connected* I became transfixed and could *not* look away. The next thing I knew, I was receiving messages in my head.

People often ask me: how do I know its Angel voices and not my imagination? The only way I can explain is this:

IT DOES NOT SOUND LIKE MINE OR ANYONE ELSE'S VOICE.

He told me he was my *Guardian Angel*.

And from now on, I would be doing my readings in a different way. At this point I noticed ALIEL had no sign of any wings.

On his second visitation I mentally asked him what his name was. The answer came back clear as a bell.

ALIEL

This is how I call him in when I need his help and guidance.

THEN, JUST AS FAST AS HE APPEARED, HE WAS GONE!!

The meeting with him had seemed like ages, but it had only been a few minutes.

When I look back now, I realise that after each of my Angel sightings a new healing modality comes into my life within a day or two.

The next vision was stronger than ever. Again while watching TV; I knew I was encountering another Angel, because of the way that he conversed with me. It was exactly the same as my previous experience.

However, his appearance was extremely different and came as a great shock to me again. This is not how I envisioned Angels would be.

Again just as before, I noticed on my left-hand side another BEING. I was in the presence of an Angel. A huge male presented himself to me, almost as tall as the ceiling; and he had a physique to match.

Aside from his unusual stature, his clothes appeared to be normal, he was wearing a white shirt and black pants, but around his neck was a stunning purple pendant, a perfect circle with a glowing white halo circling it. It was very large, and I found

"That I could not take my eyes off it."

We talked to each other mentally, nothing of an outstanding nature. But my eyes kept going back to the spectacular and hypnotising pendant that adorned his neck. It gave me the feeling of complete

Calmness

Bliss

And Tranquillity

Now I know, that when I am upset or in need of guidance, all I have to do is go back into this space, visualise the pendant, and I am quickly taken back into the feeling of completeness.

I KNEW IT WAS
A
VERY SPECIAL GIFT
THAT I HAD BEEN GIVEN

I asked for his name. But this time I was told that he is my comforter in times of upset.

Then suddenly the name **Jim** popped into my head, so I assumed that this was his name, and at that very moment…

HE WAS GONE!

Next day, a new healing modality came in; a friend invited me to a crystal workshop. I fell in love with the crystals, their vibration and their beautiful energy. I went on to teach about them for many years along with my meditation groups.

My journey had now become very interesting, and I quickly became fascinated and in awe of always learning something new on my Spiritual journey. My days and nights became filled with study as I searched for new information, knowing that I was now being guided by my Angels.

This was a completely different way of life to that I had lived as a singer on the stage entertaining people and making them happy through the joy of music.

With increasing years, the more exciting my life becomes. I am continually amazed at the way it has turned out for me, and the great blessings it has brought on my journey.

NOW ENTERS

THE

THIRD ANGEL

AND

STILL NO WINGS!!

Many years later, once again while watching TV *(I wondered why they appear while I'm watching TV, and why they choose to enter at this moment?)*. It seemed very odd that all my visitations came at this particular time, except this time he was VERY DIFFERENT.

He was tall like the second Angel, but extremely different to look at and I was now becoming aware that all my Angels were males. This one had the features of a Native American, but wearing Western gear, a checked shirt and jeans – he presented himself in the form of a shimmering shining hologram, then the name **Ted** popped into my mind, but no other words. (I have often wondered why two of them gave me ordinary names. But I never got an answer to this question.)

It was hard to take this all in. But once again, as in previous experiences, another wonderful thing happened.

A friend, Tracey Stranger, asked me to attend the book-writing workshop, called 'HOW TO WRITE A BEST SELLER' by Darren J Stephens from Global Publishing.

I had been keeping journals and writing down my experiences about my journey and my breathing techniques that I had come to learn on my Spiritual path. Not knowing that at a particular point in time it would be put to good use.

Darren accepted the manuscript, and my book *Happiness is Just a Breath Away* became a published book. My life was now becoming sheer magic – my book has taken me in directions that I could never have imagined, it has enabled me to help others while connecting me to the most wonderful people, many on their own Spiritual journey. I have never looked back and am always in awe of the magic the universe brings in when we are on the right path.

My life as a mentor and inspirational speaker has propelled me forward, with a wonderful group of friends from all walks of life helping me along the way.

Facebook has been another beneficial tool, connecting me to so many people throughout the planet, all eager to learn and teach at the same time.

To date I have not had another Angel experience of this magnitude.

Some might even think it is sacrilegious to call my visitations ANGELS, as we have been conditioned to believe that ALL ANGELS have wings, and I too always felt this was true, until my encounters, as I know they are my Angels and not my guides.

One thing that they all had was the same soft white halo around their head.

When ALIEL told me he had been with me from the day I was born and will be with me till the day I go home, I knew he was right. Looking back on my life I can see how many times his presence was there helping me even though I was not aware of it.

Many of us look back at our lives and wish that we:

Could've Would've Should've

When we see opportunities we often let go because of the fear of taking a risk. I have come to let go of the lost opportunities and appreciate what I do have and who I am now.

Years ago, like many others, I used to procrastinate when it came to doing my meditations, breathing exercises, and physical exercises – whenever I made the excuse "I'll do it when I get time" I never did.

I didn't know what to do, but one night I asked ALIEL how could I remember? As I wanted to stay healthy.

Just before the words came out of my mouth, I heard loud and clear,

"USE YOUR DIARY."

It took a while to get what he meant (to make an appointment with myself as I would be more likely to keep it).

I found it really works and it helps form a new habit.

Eventually the diary wasn't needed.

I now tell my clients to do the same, the feedback is very positive; you might like to try it yourself.

Sharing a Very Unusual But Special Experience

Every now and then when I am lying down, or I am just going off to sleep, I have what I call 'VISITATIONS'. I see several faces coming slowly into my vision towards me – just faces that look soft but serious – no smiles but the best way to describe them is the loving look in their beautiful eyes. They have never communicated; they just come close then recede again. Then another one takes the place of the other and repeats the same scenario. There are usually around five of them, I have absolutely no idea who they are, but I consider them to be guides.

What I have found after this is – 'My Day is Magic'.

They seem to appear around six month intervals, sometimes I ask them to come back, but they never do! It is always in their timing. None of them appear to be familiar, except one that is similar to my wonderful foster mother, but then, maybe that is the human in me that wants to see her.

I am mainly sharing this in case others have similar experiences.

Personal Notes

CHAPTER 3

Angelic Conversations and Messages

No Wings

Not long after Angel ALIEL introduced himself to me, I asked the leading question.

WHY DON'T YOU
HAVE WINGS?

The human in me expected a long
explanation,
But all I got was:

"WE ARE PURE LIGHT."

"WE ARE ONLY A THOUGHT AWAY."

Strangely enough, I don't receive many long conversations, most of the time it is one to three words, then I think and feel how I will put them together. The longest messages that I receive are usually when the Wisdoms and Affirmations flow.

If the Goosebumps come through, I know it is ok. If not, I tweak till they do. It is a weird but wonderful arrangement.

My two favourite answers to my many questions were to do with throat breathing and photos.

Throat Breathing

I was teaching throat breathing for many years, but most of my students couldn't understand how to connect their breathing with their throat muscles, so I asked the question, "How can I help them?"

The answer came through immediately.

SNORE!

I replied I can't do that. What else?

SNORE!

And the voice was gone.

At my next talk I told everyone to snore. They all turned and looked at each other and laughed and laughed.

Again I asked them to SNORE, so they did, then I asked them to snore silently, once again they followed my instructions, and finally they discovered the tiny throat muscles.

You see, throat breathing draws down the inflammation from the head. Our head is tightly compacted, and when we have inflammation there it creates pressure which can lead to disease, along with sinus issues, migraines, and ear nose and throat problems. Many of these may disappear when we clear the inflammation through the process of throat breathing. We swallow it in tiny bits and eventually pass it through the system.

Until we swallow, we are not doing it correctly.

Try doing this at least three times a day, about six to ten times each time, once in the mornings, then around midday, and again in the evenings. Doing this daily for approximately one month will see changes in the body as it begins to heal. Keeping this practice up throughout your life will allow your body and mind to achieve better health as you age. Your mind will think more clearly and you will make better decisions.

Discipline and Dedication is the 'KEY'.

Photos

This was quite simple but was a solution to an often-asked question.

I was getting calls from clients who couldn't remember their readings. But as I have to let it all go at the end of a reading I too didn't remember everything, and needed a solution to help them. Once again I asked the question.

HOW CAN I HELP THEM REMEMBER?

Then quite clearly I got the answer:

"TAKE PHOTOS."

My reply was, "but my camera is broken."

"Get them to take a photo of the cards with their mobile camera. This will jolt their memory and help them remember."

It works

Beautifully.

After my third Angelic vision I asked why they presented themselves in such strange ways.

Then came the answer...

We show ourselves in a way the human eye can comprehend. This allows you to focus on a form that you resonate with and can believe.

You now know that after years of visits from us, that you no longer need a form to know who we are. Your system resonates with us and you recognise us instantly.

I have been living on the Gold Coast in Australia for 59 years, it is here where I am most at home, my work here is very rewarding and brings me into contact with many beautiful souls as well as many that need guidance on this journey here on earth. Years ago I asked ALIEL another question, as I was being asked to teach others 'How to Be Spiritual'.

This was an in-depth question and I needed guidance. He told me to relay to them that they are already born

Spiritual, and that everyone already has the GOD spark residing within and it can't be taught.

'IT JUST IS.'

He suggested that I give them guidelines on how to understand the Spiritual journey and how to embrace it. Then he left.

Many of us know that we are not on a Human Journey, but a Soul Journey and once we start looking at The Kind – The Loving – The Caring and The Sharing parts of ourselves, we open up more to the Spiritual, that tiny GOD spark that resides within.

I have found that once we embrace and believe in that part of ourselves, our journey seems to open up in an amazing and beautiful way and we start to feel and act differently.

I know that for me it was as if I had opened the door to a wonderful feeling of freedom and that I could take on the world and achieve anything that I desired.

I really did feel a new surge of energy and passion within and,

"IT HAS NEVER LEFT."

Another and very interesting thing I have noticed is that my creative thinking is ten times as active and almost never stops, and of course the Angel energy backs me up all the way.

When I am doing my one on one mentoring sessions I guide others to always keep a notepad and pen with them at all times, especially when they are having their quiet moments. It is very frustrating when you can't remember your magic messages.

I myself will even leave a pad and pen outside my shower, as I am quite relaxed at this time. Angels only bring us creative ideas and messages when our mind is clear of daily clutter and worries. When our energy is positive we seem to attract others who are likeminded, then our journey steps up a notch and becomes even more exciting.

It was just after I had my first vision of ALIEL that I had a very close call while I was driving on a two-lane highway.

The sun was shining, it was a beautiful day and the traffic was flowing nicely with no problems in sight. Then in a split second there was chaos, suddenly I saw a car coming across the median strip and heading straight towards me at incredible speed. Knowing that we were going to crash, I braced myself and tightened my hold on the steering wheel and prayed. I knew we couldn't possibly stop in time.

Still heading towards me at full speed, suddenly there was complete silence; it was as if I was in a vacuum.

Then I heard ALIEL'S voice,
very calming saying

"RELAX, YOU WILL BE ALRIGHT."

Instantly the fear and panic left me and my whole body relaxed.

Suddenly I became aware of noise everywhere, the brakes were squealing, people on the sidewalk started screaming and I waited for the crash, then silence again.

'NO CRASH.'

My body could not respond for a moment, I got out of my car and my legs went to jelly. People were everywhere yelling out, "It's impossible, it's a miracle." We all went and looked at the cars and a gentleman put his business card in between the two cars and said, *"That's how close it was, but I still find it hard to believe."*

Now at this stage of my life I can still remember every detail clearly, although I cannot say that about every experience in my life.

I can still hear ALIEL'S words.

The next time he came to me I asked the question,

"Why Didn't We Crash?"

The simple answer was

"It Wasn't Your Time."

The Second Incident

A couple of years later I was on the way home, at the bottom of a steep hill turning right, with no one in sight, once again another car came at me at high speed, but this time we did crash full on. It was stranger than ever as once again it went into silence and ALIEL said:

"YOU WILL BE ALRIGHT."

This was so eerily different, as the other drivers car crashed into the side of mine with a force so great that my car lifted and started to roll over, so I braced myself as it went past the point of no return, and prepared myself to roll down the hill.

Then again stillness.

The car did the impossible and rolled back and landed heavily on its wheels, once again the same reaction of incredible disbelief from bystanders.

My car had to be towed as the motor was pushed to the other side of the car.

This time I didn't bother ALIEL with the big question. I knew:

"It wasn't my time."

Personal Notes

CHAPTER 4

Angels – Meditations and Breathing

In early days with all my innocence of Angels, I used to teach great meditations; this was due mostly to my understanding of the breath. However, once I connected with the Angel energy the magic truly began, it came in and raised my energy to a much higher vibration. I also developed a much deeper knowing of how important it is to keep our focus on one thing at a time *(this enables a much more intense and faster manifestation of learning for our higher good).*

Deep meditation with your Angels and Guides brings about deeper – fulfilling – and amazing experiences in your everyday life and Spiritual journey.

I quickly learned to focus on the counting of the breath to settle oneself and remain calm; this enables the head to clear itself of everyday clutter, while making way for a better positive energy flow, bringing higher thoughts and vibrations into our life.

I like to call my meditations 'ANGEL TIME' as I believe that when we are relaxed and fully connected we are able to receive clearer information than we do at any other time.

I don't fully connect with them until the end of my meditations, then I stay still and listen to the music and with my pen and paper in hand the writing begins to flow through me, bringing forth affirmations and wisdoms to pass onto others to help with their everyday life and their journey.

It doesn't matter how simple they are, I still write them down as they quickly disappear from my head, once I am grounded again.

I find that long, slow, gentle and deep breathing plus meditation is of *great* benefit for anyone and especially those in the natural healing industry, or for those on their Spiritual journey. Yes we can be successful without them, but even more so when you practice these two modalities together. You will most likely become much healthier, enabling you to enjoy your success as you become older, not being held back by unnecessary illnesses.

WHAT A GREAT GIFT THAT IS TO YOURSELF

The human in me finds it quite funny that I am completely deaf in one ear and three-quarters deaf in the other.

My hearing aid is extremely powerful. But the ANGEL WHISPERS are quite clear even without the hearing aid. It is as if I am hearing their words without the use of my ears.

There is another magic time to receive creative thoughts, around 3 am, others will also agree with me on this, as they too are given messages at this time of the morning. This reiterates to us, that Angels come in when the mind is calm.

I remember once asking Angel ALIEL how I could improve my meditation sessions. I received this answer back.

THE ANGEL MASSAGE

He explained to me how to go about it – get my group members to form a circle at our meditation gatherings, turn on soft music and turn front to back, then do light shoulder and back massage hardly touching each other. The lighter the better he explained.

You can try this with just 2 people as well, it is real Goosebumpy stuff.

"Tips of the fingers is enough."

Especially along the shoulders and down the back, it can also be done on the full body and fully clothed on a healing bed.

It was at this point that Elizabeth recommended the book and CD by Esther and Gerry Hicks, *Getting Into to Vortex*. The book is ok, but the CD is 'Sheer Magic'. It is more guidance than meditation.

I highly recommend it. I still use it quite often myself, and Esther has us breathing in and out bringing more oxygen into our lungs.

I suggest that you practice meditation and breathing each day, start by doing some long slow gentle breathing to relax you.

Breathe in slowly to eight counts – hold for four counts (*holding the breath cleanses the lungs*) and out for nine counts. You become calm and relaxed and doing it in nature is even more beneficial.

Years ago while I was still driving, I would go off to the beach, sit and watch the tide coming in and out. I would breathe in sync with it, and was completely amazed, feeling like I was in tune with Mother Nature. I hadn't realised that there was a rhythm to the tide, as there is with our breathing pattern, sometimes being calm and sometimes not.

Over the years of learning and teaching meditation I have tried many different styles, finding that the most enjoyable is to keep it simple – breathing in, holding the breath then letting it out. Focusing on the counting of the breath makes it much easier to clear a busy mind which never stops. I did ask my Angels how to make myself more comfortable while meditating, ALIEL came straight back with an answer

"USE YOUR OFFICE CHAIR."

I tried this and found it was a great idea, you can adjust it to a height that suits you, I am short so I lower it, it also supports the lumber, enabling you to sit straight while remaining comfortable.

It was around 20 years ago that I first decided to meditate and take up Spiritualism and self-healing. We in the Western world were just starting to discover the benefits of these modalities and finding out what our own true values are. This has been an incredible journey for someone like me, who had a normal everyday upbringing, I quickly learned how amazing our life can be once we become self-confident through deep breathing and meditation practices.

I know my connection to the universe has raised my vibration enabling me to connect more deeply with my Angels.

As baby boomers, many of us are the forerunners of the Spiritual awaking and acceptance here in Australia. Over 55 years ago I couldn't get enough of the positive thinking books written Napoleon Hill and Norman Vincent Peale. Today they are just as magical as they were then. They were way ahead of their time, just as many of us were; but the stage needed to be set.

I had no idea that the universe was preparing me for this journey of being a guide and mentor to others. I had always thought my life would be very normal and then I would pop of the planet, but as I am nearing closer to 90 it appears it is not to be so, and each day when I wake up I am ready for work and to share and help those that need my experience and my guidance.

In saying this, I am aware that my body is telling me how old it is as I am slowing down a little, but there is no pain and I am studying better than ever; with around five or six hours sleep a night. I am fully charged and ready to go and I will take a power nap during the day if I am at home. I have found that as we follow our dreams into the future we need to be even more positive about what we want and help our personal energy vibrate on a higher level.

Most of us are learning to think positively and that is making a huge difference in our lives. We really need to support our desires and intentions with

DEEP BREATHING
And
MEDITATIONS

- Your energy
- Your health
- Your creative thoughts
- Your vitality
- Your passion

All react to these two activities in a huge way to raise our 'Personal Vibration'.

Oxygen Starvation

May lead to heart attacks – Disease – Epilepsy and many other internal disorders.

Learn to Breathe Properly

And many diseases may disappear.

Many lives can be healthier and more productive if we are taught to simply breathe properly.

There is now an epidemic of aches – pain – and general fatigue amongst the population of the world.

As we breathe in more, we fill our bodies and cells with oxygen. It helps to alleviate pain and we feel and think a lot clearer.

When our mental energy is focused on containing the pain; the mind becomes foggy and it is much harder to cope with life.

It takes enormous energy to rise above pain, and then of course, there is not much left for the body to heal itself.

So it does make sense to realise extra oxygen and pranic vitality is the simple answer to most of our physical, mental and Spiritual health.

GET TO KNOW YOUR OWN BREATHING SYSTEM: VALUE IT, APPRECIATE IT AND LOOK AFTER IT.

IT IS THE ONLY ONE YOU HAVE THIS TIME AROUND.

Practicing Throat Breathing

Sit comfortably straight or lie down.

Pull your shoulders back to open up the lungs and close your eyes 'very gently'.

Just breathe normally for a while and concentrate on how air feels as it comes in through the nose.

Now with mouth closed gently, take your thoughts to the back of the throat and use the tiny muscles there to draw the breath down slowly. Then use the same muscles to gently press the air out.

Squeezing the tummy muscles as well helps cleanse the lungs and strengthen the diaphragm. Also the kidneys – spleen and all moving internal parts receive a healing massage.

It takes practice, some get it straight away, but don't give up, as I believe this is one of the best healing modalities available. Don't forget to snore silently if you can't find the throat muscles.

YOU ARE THE
POWER OF YOUR BREATH

YOU ARE THE POWER
OF YOUR MIND

USE IT WISELY

Personal Notes

CHAPTER 5

Archangels

I have had more contact with the Archangels than I do with my own personal Angels. I work constantly with the Archangels although I have never visually seen one of them. I know them by their energy and messages and they work with me in a similar manner to ALIEL, especially when it comes to the Goosebumps. The three Archangels that work with me are Michael, Raphael and Gabriel.

I had never planned to work with these three Archangels; it just seemed to happen over time, bringing me messages as my Spiritual journey grew through my daily practices.

Looking back now I can see how much harder it was for me in my early days coping with the traumas in my life, when I thought I was going it alone without any form of support. Now, as my Angels are always there for me I do not feel lonely anymore as I once did many years ago.

Archangel Michael

About Michael

Whenever I am sending prayers and blessings to others I call on Michael's energy, as I also do when I am asking for help on Mother Earth's behalf.

A lot of my friends who also work with Michael say he has all the abilities needed to co-create with us.

It Is Said

He Is the Right Hand

Of God

Archangel Raphael

About Raphael

From mine and many others own experiences Raphael is our personal doctor, and when called upon he can help with any type of healing. There are an incredible amount of healing miracles taking place when Raphael is called upon, and at times they are often instant. Looking back I have realised how long it took my body to heal and recover from pain, but nowadays with my deep connection to God and the Angels, and through utilising the power of the breath, it has enabled me to heal faster and cope with life a lot better.

FAITH HOPE AND BELIEF

This plays a big part in creating a happier more comfortable life for ourselves in every aspect of our day to day living.

It is comforting to know that we have these miraculous Angelic energies to call upon.

Archangel Gabriel

About Gabriel

I spend more time connecting with her than I do with any of the other Angels at the moment.

She is known as the Author's Angel, but her main job is to help us with our journals and any writing that we are immersed in, especially book writing.

When we have writing blocks during the course of writing a book or, our creative juices slow down, it is a good idea to walk away – take a few deep breaths and invite Gabriel in to our space, it is at this moment that we may get the answer we need or a new idea can present itself.

From my own experience and point of view, Archangel Gabriel can bring magic into our work, helping us to guide and mentor others and helping them to understand the Spiritual side of their journey while they are here on Mother Earth.

It seems that when I am using the 'power of words' by

simply calling on Gabriel, the words flow easier and more smoothly.

As I am more CLAIRAUDIENT (clear hearing) than I am CLAIRVOYANT (clear seeing), I sometimes use her energy to do my psychic readings, and then the channel of clear hearing opens up more easily, bringing in the messages that we need.

Personal Notes

CHAPTER 6

Tithings

Many years ago I wanted to write an article on 'TITHING' but for some reason I was unable to begin.

So once again I asked the ANGEL energy how I would go about explaining it.

The words flowed through 'loud and clear'.

IT IS THE UNIVERSAL LAW of giving and receiving. It is a sacred contract with the universe. Your payment in exchange for the space you occupy while you are here on the planet!

Remember, this happened when I was learning to receive my messages, and to make what I now call the simple but amazing connections.

The Energy of Tithing

The energy of tithing opens up a whole new world of abundance to ourselves as well as others – "it is a two way street."

There are many ways of tithing; for example

- Sharing your time
- Sharing your money
- Sharing your knowledge
- Sharing your wisdom
- Sharing your talents
- Sharing your love

In the end, life truly is all about 'sharing and caring', there is **'No other way'** to create true happiness on our life's journey.

Eventually we will need to open up to the absolute joy of service to others, and to do the job we were born to do.

But a word of warning here, first we need to look after ourselves so that we are then able to help others to create their own happiness.

When I am mentoring others, I am often asked why it is that when we share big time and help others that it does not come back from that same person.

I can tell you that it very seldom does, but it is more than likely to come back from another source, and is often multiplied.

Reaching Our True Potential

THERE IS A POWERFUL
GOD SPARK…

…within the human frame that keeps encouraging us to get up and try once more each time.

The worse our journey gets, the more determined some of us become, until we get to the top of the ladder. Then it is up to us to

REACH DOWN
AND HELP OTHERS.

The point is, if we don't help others once we are successful, we might lose the lot.

"IT IS THE RHYTHM OF THE UNIVERSE
IN ACTION."

Winston Churchill once gave an inspirational speech; it went like this – he walked up to the microphone and said:

"NEVER EVER – EVER – EVER – EVER
GIVE UP."

And walked off again.

The crowd went silent for a long moment; then roared with approval.

HAVE FAITH IN ABUNDANCE

AND

GIVE

GIVE

GIVE

Be brave enough and open up your heart.
To GIVE freely and JOYFULLY.
With no Expectations.
Just let it go!

The more we open our hearts to the world; its people and its animals, the more our hearts expand and receive.

The secret to LOVE – ENERGY – HAPPINESS – EVEN MONEY…

Lies in the Giving.

THE LAW OF THE UNIVERSE RELIES
ON THE BALANCE OF

GIVING AND RECEIVING

Personal Notes

ANGEL AFFIRMATIONS WITH EXPLANATIONS

CHAPTER 7

Affirmations

Are Simple but Extremely Powerful Prayers Where We are Affirming Positive Thoughts To Ourselves and the Universal Source

Choose a new affirmation daily. To be thought or said with full concentration to impress the subconscious mind. Maybe print some larger versions to place on your wall.

Somewhere where they will be seen daily or by our visitors and friends as well.

Once your subconscious mind takes it all in you might find yourself creating your own.

AFFIRMATION 1

FROM THIS MOMENT ON
I WILL NOT WASTE
TODAYS ENERGY
ON THE
NEGATIVES OF MY PAST

Explanation

This means = letting go of constantly reliving the past.

It saps our energy and prevents us becoming strong for Today's Journey.

What's more, by thinking and visiting hurts and damages in our mind done to us in the past, we are giving them permission to mentally do it over and over again.

Which prevents us being happy and successful.

AFFIRMATION 2

EVERY
DAY IN EVERY
POSITIVE WAY
I AM
BETTER
BETTER AND
BETTER

Explanation

This is an old affirmation and quote by Emile Coue. The original saying did not have the word positive. One day at the end of my meditation the thought popped in that we can even be better and better at being negative, so I always include the word positive.

Remember that the power of ONE word can make a huge difference to the outcome of your life's journey.

AFFIRMATION 3

I CHOOSE
TO ATTRACT
CREATIVE POWERS OF
THE UNIVERSE
TO HELP ME ACHIEVE
MY DREAMS

Explanation

This lets us know we can't achieve the best all by ourselves, therefore having a friend or someone to guide us or to simply listen to our dreams and aspirations can keep us on track, or sometimes Universe can send new ideas or information to guide us on our way.

AFFIRMATION 4

EVERY

SINGLE DAY

IS

A GOOD DAY

TO PRAY

Explanation

SPIRIT THRIVES ON GRATEFULNESS

A heartfelt **thank you** to the Creator – The Angels – Your Guides and all other Loving Energies each and every day helps us keep more POSITIVE and ENTHUSIASTIC.

So connecting at a deeper level helps us manifest our dreams.

AFFIRMATION 5

TODAY
I WILL LEND
A SYMPATHETIC EAR
TO SOMEONE SPECIAL

Explanation

To be a good listener is one of the greatest gifts to humanity because often a trouble shared is a trouble halved, and sometimes it can help others cope much better in life.

AFFIRMATION 6

EVERY LIMITING
THOUGHT
OF FEAR
IS REMOVED
FROM MY
CONSCIOUSNESS

Explanation

Our human mind creates fear so it will have control.

Fear is a word created to stop us taking a risk and slowing us down in case we are criticised. It stops us from stepping out of the square and from showing the world that our real value and potential is limitless.

AFFIRMATION 7

HAPPINESS
IS MY BIRTHRIGHT
IT IS NOW UP TO ME
TO CLAIM IT

Explanation

We were born to create our own happiness. The tough lessons are there to make us strong. Our true happiness is in learning to look after ourselves so we can care and share with others.

AFFIRMATION 8

I DARE
TO BE
A DREAMER OF DREAMS
BECAUSE
THIS IS WHAT CREATES MY
REALITY

Explanation

Don't let anyone stop your dreams – if you only get halfway there, it is better than not trying at all. It is your journey

No one else's.

AFFIRMATION 9

I RELEASE EVERYONE
AND EVERYTHING
NEGATIVE IN MY LIFE
I NOW
SET MY SPIRIT FREE

Explanation

Connect with your soul energy for full focus, and forgive everyone who harmed you in the past, even 'yourself'.

Don't let yourself relive negative situations from the past over and over again, or you are giving them permission to hurt you over and over again.

AFFIRMATION 10

PAST AND FUTURE
ARE NOT MY REALITY
ONLY NOW EXISTS
MY POINT OF POWER
IS
IN THE MOMENT

Explanation

Today is all that is real

Worrying about the past depletes our energy and creates nervous tension, which in turn, can make us ill, affect our relationships, and spoil our future journey. We can't change one little bit of it, so let it go and delight in moving on.

AFFIRMATION 11

TODAY
I WILL BE
THE BEST ME
I CAN POSSIBLY BE

Explanation

Maybe it's time to realise that each human being has far more potential than we know. Once we replace the negative thoughts with positive thoughts, we can fly.

AFFIRMATION 12

A
HIGH QUALITY LIFE
STARTS
WITH A
HIGH QUALITY ME

Explanation

It's not selfish to take care of myself first, because then I can take care of others *better* and *longer*.

I make good health my highest priority.

AFFIRMATION 13

I

BELIEVE IN MIRACLES

BECAUSE

I AM ONE

Explanation

The human machine is an amazing creation; it is the most incredible miracle on the planet, especially how the inside is highly organised and timed.

The breathing system, the digestive system, the heart and the brain.

Man might eventually clone a human, but he will never ever include the soul or Spirit

"THAT'S GOD'S WORK."

AFFIRMATION 14

I NOW REALISE WHAT
ABSOLUTELY
WONDERFUL POTENTIAL
I HAVE STORED DEEP DOWN
WITHIN MY TRUE ESSENCE

Explanation

It's true that we humans don't have a clue what amazing experiences we can have till we let go of fear and the worry of taking a risk.

We are fast learning to follow our gut feelings, which is our soul saying "LET'S FLY" or "DON'T TOUCH IT."

AFFIRMATION 15

THE MORE
I RELAX THE MIND
THE DEEPER
I
CONNECT WITH MY
SOUL

Explanation

Angels and Guides very seldom come in when our minds are in a worrying condition (unless in an emergency). I find that by sitting and gazing out the window at a natural scene can make all the difference, or after meditation. Just staying a while in the calm peaceful energy at the end. They might make a special connection, mine often do.

AFFIRMATION 16

I DON'T CREATE STILLNESS

STILLNESS
IS ALWAYS THERE
DEEP
DOWN INSIDE

Explanation

We just need to allow ourselves permission to make that connection.

That can happen when we FEEL it's time.

AFFIRMATION 17

I NOW
SEARCH FOR
SOLUTIONS
TO
ALL THE CHALLENGES
IN MY LIFE

Explanation

I refuse to waste my time and energy worrying about my so called PROBLEMS, no matter how bad they are. I have learned to focus and fully redirect my mind, finding the answer to improving each situation.

AFFIRMATION 18

MY ATTITUDE
TO MYSELF
IS FAR MORE IMPORTANT
THAN MY ATTITUDE
TO
ANYONE ELSE

Explanation

When we are self-critical we attract more to be critical about and that stops us going FORWARD to help ourselves and eventually help others. We need to look for the best in ourselves. The smallest things add up to feeling better, enabling us to move forward. When we are constantly self-critical we are criticising GOD'S creation, and I don't think that is fair.

AFFIRMATION 19

I BELIEVE
GOD GIVES GIFTS
AND TALENTS
TO MAKE LIFE BETTER
FOR
OURSELVES AND OTHERS

Explanation

Every single human is born with one talent or more; to help make them happy, and then they can share those talents with others so they too can be happy.

AFFIRMATION 20

TO
RECEIVE THE BEST
WE
MUST EXPECT THE BEST
AND
DO OUR BEST

Explanation

It is great to have dreams and hopes, but we can't expect to achieve them if we are not willing to do our best to help them to manifest.

AFFIRMATION 21

YOU
DON'T HAVE TO
SEE ANGELS
TO BELIEVE IN THEM

Explanation

They are simply light energy, and human energy is a feeling.

So if you don't see them, simply feel their presence.

"ASK QUESTIONS."

And sense the answer.

The first thought is usually right.

AFFIRMATION 22

DON'T THINK
SMALL
THINK
H-U-G-E

Explanation

Having been around for four generations I have had the pleasure and experience of watching the general public grow from thinking small, to learning to think big. Rhonda Byrne and her friends taught us to THINK BIG when she wrote *The Secret*. We were all so excited when we attended the workshops and started to find our own potentials and values, especially the women. We began to have freedom of thought and began valuing ourselves and others, even our 'men' more.

AFFIRMATION 23

THE
SUBCONSCIOUS MIND
IS A
POWERHOUSE
OF ENERGY

Explanation

It will MAKE you or break you, according to what you put into it.

- It does not have a sense of humour
- It does not question what you feed it
- It does not judge

It simply does its best to give you what you want.

AFFIRMATION 24

I'M TOO BLESSED
TO BE STRESSED

Explanation

Being grateful for
The small blessings each day
Helps the bigger blessings to manifest.

The last affirmation that I have created, is a set of 'THE ART OF HAPPINESS AFFIRMATIONS.'

If you practice them daily you could become Happier, Healthier and more successful.

Memorise them and when negative thoughts come in, replace them with these.

AFFIRMATION 25

THE ART OF HAPPINESS
I FEEL **WONDERFUL**
I FEEL **MARVELLOUS**
I FEEL **GREAT**

A morning affirmation when you first wake up.
Then several times throughout the day

I AM **EXTREMELY** HEALTHY
I AM **EXTREMELY** WEALTHY
I AM **EXTREMELY** WISE

An evening affirmation before going to sleep
Then several times during the day

All affirmations to be said VERY STRONGLY – OUT LOUD. No wishy washy here – thank you!

For more information visit Kawena's website
www.ExpandingEnergies.com.au

Personal Notes

KAWENA SHARES HER FAVOURITE WISDOMS

CHAPTER 8

Wisdoms

It seems to me that the true basis of happiness does come from a positive attitude, firstly towards ourselves and then towards life. I am also happy to 'see' and 'feel' more positive awareness coming into the world as we realise the need to help not only ourselves but also others.

Gratefulness is another simple tool to work with. Many of us think that wisdom automatically comes with age. The BIG news is; it doesn't.

There has always been negative energy from the beginning of time, and now it has become even more extreme. As we become aware that it is only causing more problems, we are turning it around and choosing to take care of Mother Earth, her people, and nature.

"It all comes from LOVE."

Wisdom needs to be learned and earned. I especially, have had to learn this one the hard way. We will continue to learn, to practice and to understand during the course of our lifetime on this planet.

I have often heard it said that we cannot learn everything during one lifetime, and I completely agree with this.

WE ARE PURE
ENERGY
AND MOST OF US
EITHER AREN'T AWARE OF
OR
SIMPLY DON'T APPRECIATE
WHAT **MAGNIFICENCE**
IS LOCKED DOWN DEEP
INSIDE OF US

BUT
WE DO GET THE **FEELING**
THAT THERE IS
SOMETHING SPECIAL
WE HAVEN'T TAPPED INTO AND
WE DON'T KNOW
WHERE TO **START**

I have been observing how quickly we have advanced in our thinking and how many souls are taking advantage of this amazing age of information.

We are finally finding our passions and fulfilling them.

THE WORLD IS
LITERALLY
OUR OYSTER

Most of us are now feeling the new surge of energy rippling through the planet, and we are eager to be part of it.

So many of us are searching as to why we are here and what is our true I.D.

Even those who weren't interested before are becoming inquisitive as they are seeing many of us making ourselves happy, contented and successful, 'no matter what'.

This is a big deal, and we are finally shouting from the hilltops (sometimes via Facebook) and we are proud of our incredible Spiritual journey.

So let's be:

BRAVE ENOUGH: To show affection.

BRAVE ENOUGH: To speak our truth (diplomatically).

BRAVE ENOUGH: To follow our dreams (peacefully).

and

SMART ENOUGH: To look after our precious planet for ourselves and the children of the future.

WISDOM 1

In the Wisdom of Sitting Quietly

Think about how many of the Spiritually minded people are the NEW Driving Force for change on Planet Earth, and that now it is up to us to help this beautiful planet we call home.

Through the simple act of sharing the energy of love and caring we feel the change that most of us knew was coming.

Over the four generations that I have been here, I have watched many traditions come and go and I find that this New Age of information given to us allows us to value and understand ourselves and others more than we have at any other time in history.

This year of 2017 is expected to be a magical year, so lets us all focus on achieving our dreams, thus putting ourselves in the position to help other achieve their goals and dreams.

KNOWLEDGE is POWER
BUT we need to use it wisely.

WISDOM 2

Wisdom is a pearl beyond price
By spreading your knowledge
You are sharing
Your wisdom and talents
and helping make
The world a better place
So lighten up
By sharing your
LOVE
LIGHT
AND
LAUGHTER
Then you will attract
A new circle of likeminded friends

WISDOM 3

You Will Find

There is amazing energy
And power
Behind every word
You think or speak

So you need to make sure
That every word
Is a productive one
Not
A destructive one

WISDOM 4

Give
To the utmost
And your rewards
Will take care of
Themselves

Not always in
The same form
Or from the same
Direction
But in ways you could
Never imagine

WISDOM 5

Gratitude
Is the
Language
Of
The heart

Let your heart
Express
Itself today

WISDOM 6

Lend

A sympathetic ear

To someone special

A GOOD LISTENER

Is

One of the greatest

Gifts to humanity

WISDOM 7

When

Good people

Say Nothing

Nothing good

Gets done

It's time to speak your

Truth

But do it diplomatically

And don't hurt others

WISDOM 8

Self-Care

A high quality
Life
Starts with a
High quality **You**

It's **not** selfish to
Take care of
Yourself first
Because
Then you can take
Care
Of others better

WISDOM 9

A little bit
Of love goes a long way
And comes back
Tenfold

Often from the most
Unexpected places

So be brave and
Share your
Love

WISDOM 10

LOVE

Is the

Fulfilment of the

Universal law

And

Faith is the

Energy that opens

The CHANNEL

WISDOM 11

If we don't teach (share) what we learn, we stifle the rhythm of life.

This means that it is a privilege and a gift to be willing to pass on your knowledge during your lifetime.

By spreading your knowledge and talents across the planet much more satisfaction and happiness comes to us. This can be simply sharing and caring.

"It is the key to happiness."

IT ALWAYS HAS BEEN

We are now becoming aware of our own possibilities and potential. So open up and be BOLD and begin to go forward. We can do it, it just takes…

THAT FIRST STEP.

The main thing to remember is, it's ok to make mistakes. We were born to do just that so we can learn lessons and become stronger.

WISDOM 12

Don't expect others
To make you happy
It's not their job
It's yours

Their job is to make
Themselves happy
Then when two happy people
come together
That's the icing on the cake

WISDOM 13

= The Magic of a Tree =

As I sat at my desk I was waiting for inspiration, as to what I should write about for Kawena's Weekly Wisdom…

There is a huge tree in the distance outside my window that I love to sit and look at every day.

Suddenly I realised that there is my inspiration.

This majestic tree stands there in all its Glory; year in and year out putting up with whatever life has to offer it; no matter what.

Sometimes powerful winds attack it and tear off its branches and leaves. Then the storm brings rain and hail and yet it still stands its ground; and in spite of it all, when the trees season comes around, some trees burst into bloom in all their glory for us to admire and appreciate. Other trees bring fruit, nuts and berries while others show us the beauty of a new growth of leaves.

But the main job of absolutely every tree on Mother Earth is to provide us with oxygen for every living thing on the planet; including us. For trees have the most important job there is.

Maybe it is time to focus on them, appreciate them, Value them and enjoy them more than ever.

I KNOW I WILL – WHAT ABOUT YOU?

Blessings to our friends the trees.

Personal Notes

CHAPTER 9

The Energy of Colour

Colours are one of the greatest energies available; simply just looking at colours that we either like or don't like, can change our mood for the day. However, I do notice that, even if I only have a splash of colour on a neutral background (grey, fawn, brown, or navy) etc., I feel great, but if I look in the mirror and see only the basic neutrals my day is not quite as exciting.

It is as if what my eyes are seeing is transferred to my feelings, and my energy goes down.

When I was a young girl, I remember that we weren't allowed to wear bright colours – only what were referred to as 'Ladies of the Night' did that, and you were labelled as being cheap if you wore bright colours.

When I was learning to sing around middle age, I was very shy and it didn't take much to make me blush. When I eventually became brave enough to perform on stage we were all dressed in bright colours and my confidence began to grow and I then became quite ambitious.

I advise the use of colour within the home; it helps lift your Spirit and that of others. Some of Gods most beautiful creations are the colourful flowers, butterflies, birds, animals and fish, their colours can uplift our Spirit and brighten our day. Gemstones are another wonder of God.

Yes I do believe colour plays a big part in our lives, it would be awful if everything was in black and white.

Colour therapy is also used by many healers to heal the body and the chakra system.

Hospitals are also using colour to cheer up their patients. I am so pleased that this generation embraces colour. Department stores and restaurants value colour also, people feel wonderful when they enter and see it.

We use bright colours to party and celebrate.

SO WHY NOT CELEBRATE EVERY DAY WITH THE COLOURS WE LOVE

About the Aura

This is such a fascinating subject, but we will never know it all. What we do know is that the aura is the energy field around the body and all living things. The healthier the aura the more energetic and vitalised we are, we don't feel the same stress as we do when the energy is low and our aura is weak. If the aura is weak we become tired, nervous and depressed. Then we find it hard to create positive experiences in our life.

Control of our personal energy via THE POWER OF THE BREATH and THE POWER OF THE MIND gives us a better chance to create an amazing healthy aura and happiness.

The Aura Layers

The Aura has seven layers, which are incorporated into the following:

- The Electromagnetic layers. Vibrates to the base Mental, Emotional and Physical vibration of the body.
- The Etheric body, Higher, Mental and Emotional states.
- The Astral body represents the Spiritual aspect of us.

Aura Colours

The aura is the most amazing energy colour of all. The colours help us react to our health, our thoughts, and our Spirit and to the amount of oxygen we breathe in.

The aura fluctuates – vibrates and never stays the same for long, changing colour with each situation in our daily life. Everything that we are is contained with our aura.

At the time of death, I feel that this is the part of us that goes home, leaving the physical body behind.

I don't get annoyed much, but when I hear people say to mediums

"YOU TALK TO DEAD PEOPLE."

I feel like telling them!

NO THEY DON'T

THEY TALK TO

THE PERSONS SPIRIT

The dead body is buried or cremated.

Have you ever walked into a crowded room and automatically chosen to walk to a particular group of people? You may have felt the positive energy emanating from their auras, or you have walked into an empty house and had cold chills, or maybe even a soft warm feeling, this is because past energies are stuck there, whether it is a feeling of happiness, joy, sadness, or a negative vibration.

We can cleanse a house thoroughly when the energy is low, with candles, sage and prayer, go into a deep meditation and ask the energies to go and that they have permission to move on.

I have also used brightly coloured squares of felt – I would place them around the room, and it would raise my own vibration allowing me to connect more fully with these energies. Speaking out loud rather than just thinking the words helps to make a stronger connection, it seems simple but has always worked for me.

Crystals and the Aura

Wearing our favourite crystals or gems can energise and revitalise the auric energy.

The aura allows the energy from the stone to filter through to the physical body. This can encourage healing and intuitiveness to be stronger.

It is a wise move to take any crystals or gems that are not compatible out of your bedroom if you can't sleep.

Les

A near death experience.

I remember before I was ever on my Spiritual journey, my then husband fell from a tree and crushed two vertebrae along his spine. As he was coming out of the operation he started yelling and rolling around in his bed. He was yelling out!

"I DON'T WANT TO GO BACK,
I DON'T WANT TO GO BACK"

And then he woke up. The nurses asked him what happened. Then he started to settle and told them.

“I was walking along a white road, and on both sides were rows of the most colourful flowers I have ever seen, the colours were so strong and bright, I had trouble looking at them, and they were pulsating with a life force of their own.”

He said, “I kept walking towards the pure snowy white ray of light in the distance, and as I got closer there was a huge golden door in front of me. I knocked on the door, and a very deep voice said…

(Voice) What do you want?

(Les) I want to come in

(Voice) You can’t come in

(Les) Why not?

(Voice) You have to go back; you still have work to do

(Les) So here I am and I feel heavy!”

The Salvation Army

Les had never been into religion, actually none of us had. After his recovery, he went on to become a charity worker and collector for the Salvation Army. He always remembered the vibrancy of the flowers during his NDE, and said the flowers on earth were extremely dull in comparison.

Personal Notes

CHAPTER 10

Cleansing Prayer

In the name of GOD I invoke that a grounded Healing
Be activated throughout the whole of this house,
Rendering it fit for human habitation.
May all negative energies be blessed,
Released and taken care of.
I ask that the white light of the universe cleanse,
Energise and fill this home with the miracle of
Light and Love.
To be felt by everyone residing in or visiting
this special place.
From this day on I ask the Universal Source,
To provide this home and its occupants with
The blessings of Love
The blessings of Health
The blessings of Happiness
Thank you
Amen

The Birth of the Cleansing Prayer

In the year of 2005 I was awakened around 3 am with a statement in my head, so I got out of bed on this cold winter's night and wrote it down, knowing that if I didn't it would be gone in the morning.

The previous day I had been to a workshop, learning about smudging and the clearing of negative energies. Therefore I sensed that my Angel ALIEL felt this would be a good time to bring me the following prayer.

I had heard from others that they too receive creative messages at this unearthly hour of the morning.

I get great feedback from this prayer, so write it down and I also suggest remembering it off by heart.

You can go to my website where you will also find it. You might like to put it in your home or as a gift to others.

www.ExpandingEnergies.com.au
https://www.facebook.com/KawenaGordon

SECTION 2

The Experiences of Others With Their Angels and Guides

CHAPTER 11

Guides and Their Influence

By Dr Linet Amalie

I was born a psychic medium; I have always believed that I am looked after by my Spirit Guides and I am very aware of how they can help us.

My main Spirit Guide is a sixteenth century apothecary (pharmacist). She helps me in my work as a medical intuitive giving me the assistance I need to help my clients to identify and prevent any potential illness that may occur in their life. She supported me throughout my basic hospital training giving me answers with my exams and would practically 'nudge' me when someone was going to pass over, guiding me into their room to give comfort.

She helps me connect to the Universe when I undertake mediumship work and is a filter when other peoples' loved ones come knocking at inappropriate times wanting to talk to me.

How do we know when our Spirit Guides are trying to make contact with us?

The signs can be very subtle or sometimes in your face and lifesaving if you take the time to notice them. I met some of my Spirit guides many years ago. They all make contact with me in different ways.

One of them has an unusual habit of 'pushing me in the back' when I am about to make, or have made, a poor decision. I physically feel a light 'nudge' around my upper back and shoulder area. This Guide was a male, quite active and from England, he told me he travelled to America in the early 1920s and was run over by a trolley car when on business. He told me he was just an 'average guy' with no special talents, but did like soccer.

My other Guides also help me in my day-to-day life; another was as an elderly lady who spent her time in the early nineteenth century travelling the world on cruise ships. She had a penchant for fine food, wine and luxury living. She told me that she died whilst on one of these luxury cruises and her job is to help me source quality items when I make purchases of expensive clothing, furniture or cars – she always guides me to the right shop saving me time as well as leading me to the quality product which will last me a *very* long time and saves me money.

Another Guide I have was a physically strong Polynesian Islander from the 1700s who drowned whilst being transported on a slave boat which sank in a storm. Even though he was a swimmer and a brave warrior he was unable to survive the shipwreck. He guides me to find strength, calmness and peace when I am feeling overwhelmed and has given me my appreciation and love for nature including activities such as hiking and swimming.

Arranging and Nudging

Guides can also nudge you in the direction they want you to go and are able to arrange for something good to happen for you.

I met this next Guide during a regression therapy training workshop in America, discovered her history, and how she had helped me 35 years ago during my very first visit to America. This female Guide was from a small town in upstate New York in America and lived in the 1930s and 40s. She gave me full details of her name and address and the suburb she moved to when she married and moved to New York City during the war.

She told me that during her time on earth, she worked as a junior secretary and typist in an office working in the city; she was happily married and then lived by herself in an apartment when the war started as her husband had joined the armed forces, and was shipped out to fight in Europe. She told me that on her way to work one day she fell downstairs in a subway station breaking her lower ankle and leg; complications then set in as the bone was quite badly shattered and subsequently the wound became infected, she contracted gangrene from this injury and passed away from the blood poisoning.

She told me that 25 years ago, when I first went to New York, she was the one who helped me find the

Backpackers Hostel that I needed when I had no money, my belongings had been stolen and was feeling quite lost, scared and alone.

I am from Australia and had no knowledge about New York, I asked the person who transgressed me at the time to confirm these geographical details she talked about, and it was confirmed that this train station had closed just after the war, and the suburb she came from did indeed exist in the State of New York.

Even though I didn't know her all those years ago, I always wondered how I knew to walk in the right direction and which street to go down to find the accommodation in that small side street. Now I knew, I thanked her; she was, at that point in time 'The Guide' behind the scenes helping when I needed vital assistance.

I also met my husband because of one of these psychic 'arrangements and nudges'. We had previously been a couple many years before as young adults; we then went our separate ways, married and had children. I had no contact with him for many years, as I believed he was still married and living with his children interstate, I often thought about him from time to time, wondering how his life had turned out.

A mutual friend then contacted me when one of his relatives passed away and sent me his details. I suddenly felt this overwhelming urge to contact him to send my condolences, I did this discovering that he also believed I was still married and wondered how my life had turned out. He informed me he was single and had actually been trying to contact me for a while. My Guides were at work to help us reunite, definitely not a coincidence!

Personal Notes

CHAPTER 12

The Archangels and My Angel Experiences

By Julia Anais

I believe there have been many times that I have felt the presence of Angels. I mostly feel the energy working through me and around me; it is a warm, loving and very comforting feeling. I find it difficult to explain, however once the awareness settles within, you realise you just know.

I have had one experience of an actual vision when I was visited shortly after my grandmother passed away. One evening suddenly a full body vision of my grandmother appeared in front of the inside of the window: I recall the detail of her face and hands clearly, her body was covered by a sheer flowing white fabric as she hovered in mid-air and seemed to be surrounded by a green-like aura. I didn't feel fear at all, in fact it was quite a calm and loving experience and I felt she was letting me know she was at peace.

My next recollection of an Angel experience was when my father was very ill and nearing the end of his life. I was in the hospital room and felt an enormous energy of warmth, calm and love on that day, shortly before he passed – there was only myself and him in the room, however I felt surrounded by this energy and recall thinking how beautiful and peaceful it felt despite the circumstance we were in. It was quite unusual and somewhat overwhelming, though reassuring at the same time. It was several years later as my Spiritual Journey guided me, that I came to understand this was the energy of the Angels presence to guide him home.

Another sign that has become a regular occurrence has been finding feathers at the most synchronistic moments. I came to know the relevance of these being from the Angels after attending a Spiritual Development Course. At that time I was given advice to understand how the Angel signs work, and which encouraged me to notice the synchronicity. I learnt more about the meaning of the colours of the feathers to understand the relevance of the messages. In time I also became aware of repeating number sequences which began mostly with 11.11. The messages in those, based on numerology, further guided me. With my understanding, both feathers and numbers now contribute greatly to the guidance I receive in everyday life.

I had an opportunity to appear within a Spiritual Group, offering an experience of hosting the Angel energy in my home; I decided it felt like a lovely thing to do. The task was to create an altar with a white flower, a candle and an apple, as well as some written goals to have the Angels work with for several days. This included a ritual for welcoming the Angels and a ritual for closing the space and releasing the Angels to the next pre-chosen hosts. Strangely I found I could really feel the presence of the Angels. My children questioned the feelings they were noticing and commented on changes they felt in our home. One of my boys actually found he had dreams to do with this altar which brought him some guidance. It really seemed to restore calm to many areas of our home and family life. This was rather an incredible experience, with unexpected powerful energy shifts that I have felt somehow contributed to the overall balance of energy in our home. The space where the altar was set has been one that has seemed to continue to have an energy, and actually some 18 months later I was guided to set up a desk for the purpose of beginning the writing of my own book, I find often in that space I am greeted with instant guidance.

For me, the most remarkable example of the Angel presence and help given was when I had a health emergency – suddenly one day I found my body thrown into chaos. The event which unfolded can only be explained as frightening, as without warning a very intense dizzy spell sent my heart racing and I knew something was very wrong, I had never experienced anything like it before. Somehow I remained in a calm state, without panicking, and intuitively directed those around me to get me to the help I needed. I recall feeling very peaceful. I had the strangest sense of believing I would be ok; it felt like I was in a cocoon. I found as I experienced an intense heart rate surge, with my eyes closed, I was completely surrounded by a bright white light and although aware of everything going on, I still didn't feel fearful, there was quite a serene and powerful energy around me. I was aware the doctors were very concerned at that point sending my hubby out of the room. I communicated telepathically, "Please let me stay, please make me ok, I need to be here for my family as I haven't finished on this journey." I felt overwhelming warmth and recognised this as the Angels presence and then suddenly my body was totally at ease. It was a very serious event, however, I truly believe I was wrapped in the Angel's care.

Sightseeing in New York, my family and I were taking a walk through Central Park, it was a dreary rainy day and we were soaked. We took shelter at a pleasant boat house cafe for a warming drink by the log fire. Sitting around the table chatting; our conversation turned to sharing ghostly stories, I felt a change in the energy. As we left this cosy space to head back out to drizzly weather and continue our walk, we all agreed we had spooked ourselves a little. Making our way along the path we stopped to take photos, afterwards I noticed a hazy figure appearing with us, this had not been in any of the pictures taken earlier before our stop. I could actually feel this energy following us and know it was my father… joining us in our adventure and family pictures, so delighted to feel his presence.

Another experience connecting me to the Spirit world was on a visit to Barcelona. This trip was brought to me in a most magical way by winning a competition. I feel very certain the travel to this very old city was meant for me, the whole experience felt guided by the Angelic realms and was steeped in Spiritual connections. The most prominent connection was when visiting a fountain in the centre square of very old buildings, one which had been an orphanage and school, back in the early 1800s. This site, tragically, during the war had a bomb land on it and many of the occupants, mostly children, had died. I could feel the deep sorrow surrounding me in the square where I stood near the centre fountain.

Walking away from the area out through a side alley, I was startled when suddenly I became overwhelmed with emotion, tears prickled my eyes and I felt nauseous; it was a very intense feeling, very eerie. For a short distance, as I continued to walk away, this feeling remained, my hubby noted a physical change in me and saw I had turned very pale in my face. This became obvious to me also when a bit further around the corner I stopped to pose for a photo at a little perfume shop named Julia… I looked like I had seen a ghost! It was an odd experience, one I felt through my entire body.

On returning home from my travels, recounting this event to a psychic friend, I was advised I clearly had an entity pass through me. I feel a strong connection to children and believe my presence attracted this lost departed Soul.

I regularly feel the presence of Angel energy in daily life and often find I am strongly guided by my grandmother, who as you have read, visually appeared to me many years ago. Recently in times of extreme changes happening in my life, and finding the upheaval very challenging, I had again been noticing her obvious energy around me. When I took a couple of photos of a grey sofa bed I had been sleeping on, to my surprise I discovered the photos turned out with a pink colour in the form of someone sitting, this was not visible looking at the sofa but showed up in both photos, I was amazed though once again delighted.

The presence of Angels never brings fear, though difficult to comprehend, I have so many confirmations of the existence of this powerful energy and truly believe we can all embrace and feel the strength of this unconditional love within our hearts.

The Angels' presence has made the greatest difference to my life; I find I feel constantly supported by a greater energy. I also find I am easily uplifted by the smallest signs and confirmations… it is a magical experience.

Julia

Personal Notes

CHAPTER 13

My Support Team

By Sonia Crystella

I was born into a family of spiritually aware people; my older brother would wake up in the middle of the night talking to people in his room, and my younger sister would retrieve dead insects; performing a little ritual she would try to bring them back to life. That was the 1950s and 60s and it was not something you could talk about; without raising concerns about your psychological state. These days it is a completely different story, we are waking up and wanting to know more.

It is funny how Angel encounters and visitations come at the most unexpected moments in our lives and the most timely moments – they appear before us in various shapes and forms, in a way that we can comprehend, they have an extremely high vibration and their true self is not always recognisable to us in the human world. We are programmed from a young age as to what Angels are supposed to look like. Once you connect with them you will come to sense when they are near; their energy is completely different to our guides.

My first encounters of nonhuman forms that I can remember; came at a very young age, when I was around three years old. I was hounded by lower vibration energies and lost souls as a small child; never understanding why, or who they were, except that I was often frightened. I would crawl on my hands and knees up the hallway to my parent's room, and climb into bed with them; terrified of the monsters (as a three-year-old me liked to call them). In time I came to realise; that to do the spiritual work I was here to do, being thrown in the deep end was the only way I would learn *(this reiterates that we very often learn and become strong the hard way).*

We are all here to do different jobs, not only in the physical world but also on the spiritual path, and I was going to need a lot of help to do the job I had signed up to do, or the job that GOD had given me to do. Over time my support team has taught me to sense who and what these energies are (through feel and vibration).

You could liken spiritual work to working in a supermarket, the checkout operators, the stackers, the butchers, the manager, the cleaners and the helpers all contributing, no one is more important than the other; everyone is playing their part to achieve an end result.

The monsters made perfect sense to me, when at the age of 59 years, and then again at 60 years of age, during two healing sessions, the healers relayed to me the various encounters I had endured as a child and how they have impacted on my life, bringing me to a place of understanding energy as well as my own life purpose.

So what is the difference between The Angels – Our Guides – the Star Beings and Multidimensional Beings?

They, like us, are playing their part in this vast multidimensional universe, they have their roles within different dimensions, helping to raise the vibration and bringing us closer to LOVE. What we need to do is stay grounded and balanced when we have unexplained visits and experiences from the Angels – Light Beings and other energies.

I am sure those of you that have had encounters throughout your life will understand, it can be unsettling at first, and not something everyone can come to terms with.

Most humans focus on day-to-day living, not wanting to give any thought as to what this planet might be about – it is easier for the majority to not face the truth, as once you understand the spiritual journey your life takes on a whole new meaning, your priorities change and you start questioning all that we have been conditioned to believe as real.

I tried to turn my back on this path, living a life of materialistic wants and needs while trying to block it all out. (It never worked for long.)

Throughout the years I have met people from all walks of life who have these experiences – we are not drug-taking hippies, and many of us choose to be vegetarians, do not drink alcohol, or take painkillers, as they are quite often a distraction, and in many cases are a hindrance to our spiritual vibration and its progress.

I have come across lawyers, business professionals, including doctors and nurses, and some of the extremely wealthy, who like the rest of us walking the spiritual path, are here to help. There is no one shoe fits all for this type of work, although at some point many gravitate to spiritual work as a day-to-day job.

There needs to be balance on this planet, though at times it doesn't appear to be so, and many of us wonder; what is the reason for the work that we do here on earth, not only our own journey, but that of others who are also trying to make sense of it?

This is where the Angels and Guides can be of great importance and support to us.

Love

What I have learned on my journey and from my support team is; without love and compassion we would crumble. It is the only saviour for humanity, which is why many of us are here, and why the Angels, Masters, Star Family and Guides support us – they know this is not an easy planet to reside on, but they are here to help us in times of need and growth, whether we are facing positive or negative situations, while at the same time prompting us to wake up, be true to ourselves and do what we can to look after the planet.

From a young age I would leave my body at night and fly, something a lot of children do, that is, until they tell family members who ridicule them for believing these experiences and encounters are real, telling them it is nonsense, then many of the children shut down, until a trigger opens them up again.

Not everyone has 'Winged Angel' experiences, some have multidimensional experiences where they connect with other dimensional realities (this is something I did many times), encountering Light Beings and other Beings with and without human forms.

I get on with my life while at the same time doing the spiritual work of transmuting energy with the help of my support team, and anchoring light grids for planetary healing. I have cleared land and energies in several countries, where the energy is dense and heavy and where portals open up. Balancing and harmonising the environmental layout is paramount, it allows others to reside in a peaceful space. I have questioned many of the things I have seen and experienced, but they are always reinforced by follow up confirmations.

Many years ago my then partner and I were getting married in Las Vegas and we were staying at the Luxor in the Pyramid. It was the night before our wedding; he was not a spiritual person, but he had seen enough to know other realms were very real, woke up screaming and swearing at someone; he told me the Angels were telling him that he was not to marry me or they would intervene. Two years later at a Doreen Virtue seminar a girl turned to me; relaying a message from the Angels she said; "*You must leave your husband. He is holding you back from fulfilling your life purpose.*" I was very annoyed; to me, he was the man of my dreams. Ten days later my marriage came to an abrupt end. Once I worked through the pain, I came to realise that I was being protected.

Do we listen or trust enough to act on these messages? Unfortunately the human in us won't always accept this, so we repeat mistakes until we do learn.

My guide Ming Sui is with me when I go out of my body to do soul rescue work. He once stood me before a spiritual mirror and removed my cloak, revealing my energy as gold light. The human side of me didn't accept this; I always felt my auric field was bluer, but who am I to question what the higher realms show me?

Archangel Michael is also with me whenever necessary as I clear land buildings and energy. He is a powerhouse of love and energy; he stands on my left hand side, he is here to help all who call on him. He will hand me his sword at various times to cut away energy, he comes in through 'The Energy of the Blue Ray'.

My ancient Hebrew Angel Na'chya is also forceful and strong, but always in the name of love, he has taught me to be like this when sending energy to the light, never fearing anything that needs transmuting through love and compassion.

The light language that comes out of my mouth never fails to amaze me, but in the same breath I don't find it strange but rather normal. I am very analytical and once questioned this language, asking Na'chya why it wasn't in English. His answer to this was; *it will weaken the vibration when clearing energy.*

I understood immediately.

I am surrounded by a powerful band of Angels and Star Beings.

So do any of them have wings?

Yes and no; there are times when Michael wraps me in his wings, I feel and see this as energy and colour rather than feathered wings. I feel his beautiful presence and his power; he is filled with a LOVE so great that my whole body goes into complete stillness. I asked him about Angel wings and what they are used for, as I knew they didn't need wings to move from place to place. He told me they are a shield of protection (protection for us when needed, or when we call on their help); it made a lot of sense.

"The Angel energy is pure love with no agendas."

The Blue White Light Beings come to me in Light form and connect with me through my higher heart chakra and third eye, presenting their nonhuman form – their light is bright and extremely calming. They reinforce to me why I do this work and how it will be used at a later date to help teach others; especially where energy is concerned and its impact on every aspect of our life.

The Masters and Star Tribes are also a constant support, without these Powerful Beings of LOVE I would feel lost. They have made me a better person, and also taught me self-respect, self-love and healing of the inner child. They have also connected me to higher aspects of myself. It has allowed me to see that we exist on many levels.

My mother, who was very connected to Mother Earth and is now on the other side, is often around me helping with my journey. It is interesting to observe the changes in loved ones energy once they transcend back to the Light.

Don't forget our beautiful pets who have passed, they are also by our side, and at times, you will catch them through your peripheral vision.

But where there is Light so is there Dark; I am completely aware there is Yin and Yang and that we need both to exist, both positive and negative are part of existence. Finding a balance is the best thing we can do for ourselves, not letting the human emotion of fear take control.

There is so much that we do not understand, but we continue to learn and to grow. Now there are teachers here to help us as we step out on this journey, as well as guiding the new children that have incarnated here to help heal the planet and her occupants; these children need to know it is alright to be themselves and not cover up who they truly are; they are aware, highly sensitive, and can find it hard to adjust to Earths frequency – their DNA is different and these special children need encouragement and understanding as they fulfil their life purpose. If you know of children like this, please assist them and their parents to find the right people to help them. Asperger's Syndrome, Autism and ADHD are also signs that some of these children display. I wish this information was available and common knowledge when I was a child.

Years ago when I was very young I needed more answers; I also felt different to others and didn't know where to turn, so I visited a Spiritual church. I was tired of hearing spiritual people saying they only had beautiful Angelic and spiritual encounters, while telling me that I must be negative to have these other experiences. The Reverend took me aside and explained that I am doing a job that is important and one I should not be afraid of or fear. It is the fear that gives power to negative energy, both human and nonhuman. It was at this point that everything changed; I allowed my support team to teach me ways to clear energies, sending them to a place of healing and transformation. Now that is positive!

The Violet Flame is another energy source that everyone should utilise; St Germain's Violet Fire is one of the most healing and cleansing energies available to us as humans, and one I use daily during my meditations, clearing my chakras; and when I feel I am around energies/people that are draining. My family of light has taught me to use energy and blessings in my daily life, from the food I eat, to the people and situations I encounter.

Repeating the words below, whenever necessary; will help keep your energy field clear as you go about your day. It is not a mantra but rather a statement that identifies a fact.

"I Am a Being of Violet Fire; I Am the Purity GOD Desires."

Everything is composed of energy, it comes in many different forms both physical and nonphysical, when we tune in and trust our Higher Self, and our family of Light, we come to understand it through our finely tuned senses.

Seeking out likeminded people will support us as we grow on this journey, even if it is to talk about the things we see, feel and hear, will help us to understand GOD'S plan a little better and to know that we are supported, loved, and not alone.

Blessings

Personal Notes

CHAPTER 14

My Angels

By Leila Dal-Zotto

The rain outside is making nature smile. The leaves glisten as the raindrops fall gently upon them, everything now looks so fresh and cleansed. I realised in that moment, that that is how I feel when I have had an Angelic experience, lighter, brighter, and a complete sense of peace, as if all concerns before then have been washed away.

"Just Pure Love."

Now of course it is up to me in my humanness how long that stays, how long it will take before I get back into the thought processes that take me away from being pure love.

These days I mainly see an Angel presence in my mind's eye whilst I am also receiving messages for me and others.

They appear to me as white flowing beings with wings, often I see hints of colour around them which helps me to distinguish one from another, if I don't quite hear the name I don't always know who it is. However the love and peace that fills the room is a beautiful feeling to accept.

If I am in a session with a client an Angel will appear near them, I then let them know they have an Angelic connection. Sometimes the client will reply that they have been trying to connect with the Angels or have been calling them for help.

It is wonderful confirmation for them. When we are graced with the presence of Angels, the way they appear can be as individual as the information they give.

Two of my Angelic experiences have been profound and life changing. For the first, I need to go back to 1981–82. I was a young single mother who had just moved back to Victoria to show her first born off to friends and estranged family. I possibly even thought it might improve things within the family dynamic. My father had only two girls and I thought no matter how things were, he would be happy to have a grandson around, and I was right.

I knew what love and joy this little one had brought into my life, he was my everything, my love, my light and my heart emerged with his.

One day the unimaginable thing happened, there was a terrible accident at home, and my beautiful boy was very hurt and was rushed to hospital. My world was shattered, I did what I had to do to get to him every day, but I started to withdraw into myself.

I wasn't brought up religiously, but if there was a time to start praying it was now. I was in my bedroom asking God to please heal my son, and for whatever reason if he needed to be scarred, please do not let it be his face. He was the cutest blond blue-eyed boy with the biggest smile. I was talking/praying how my son had shown me what love is, when I heard a voice very clearly say: "He will be healed."

It was then that I looked up; on my wall was a painting of a male Angel. I thought I was seeing things, the Angel moved, I then realised the significance of prayer, again I heard:

"He will heal in ways unexpected, trust in you."

It was the case, and his little face healed without a mark on it.

The doctors had told me that he would be in and out of hospital, but that was not the case, it was like a miracle had occurred.

Another profound experience came with the meeting of one of my guides, I still feel so blessed when I think about it. One day I thought it would be a nice change to take my meditation group to listen to someone else's group. While we were sitting in the circle the gentleman came over to me and offered me a healing, as Spirit had asked him to do so, and I told him about the work I was doing with others.

He then laughed and said, "We won't take no for an answer."

I knew then he was being guided, it was during that healing that I saw the brightest light I had ever seen, and have seen to this day.

I couldn't work out how it could be so bright and not hurt my eyes. I felt a presence behind the light and just when I thought I could see something or someone, the light got brighter. I was told many things, and it was so amazing. I then started to see big clear block letters appear in front of me "METATRON." It was 20 years ago and I thought it was the name of a planet. My now ex-husband did research and discovered it was the Archangel who sits closest to God. This is often controversial, as many think it is Archangel Michael.

I love and work with both of them; I know and experience their energies in different and subtle ways and trust in their connection.

I wish you all much love and Angel blessings.

Lovingly Leila

Personal Notes

CHAPTER 15

Who Said That?

By Karen Wilson

On holiday in Western Australia I sat in the backyard of a friend's house gazing at the night sky. It was still and clear, the stars that looked like fairy lights on a Christmas tree.

As I enjoyed the moment, someone from behind me spoke.

"You are not learning this for yourself."

"Learning what," was the first thing I thought as I turned around to see who'd spoken. There was no one there; so the first thing I had wondered was, who said that? The voice was crystal clear and very matter of fact. The remark was totally random, thinking about it, the only thing I could connect it to be was a reflexology course I had recently completed. That was in 2002, and it is the first recollection I have of hearing this voice. In hindsight it was a pivotal moment. It's as if that one comment opened the door for me to connect with Spirit on a whole new level.

Since making itself known 15 years ago this is a voice I have come to know well. I have never been one to stand on ceremony, and communicating with it is no exception. I don't feel a need to establish its name or what it looks and it doesn't seem bothered by that. Occasionally it speaks out of the blue like it did on that very first night. It draws my attention to something or suggests something I should do. Other times when I'm thinking about something it pipes up with an opinion. It guides me, prompts me, and occasionally even laughs at me. While sometimes sounding quite stern it is always loving, supportive and instructional.

Over the years and since that night in Scarborough, my connection to Spirit has grown. Back then I already knew I wanted to transition from corporate work to a career in healing of some type. Various courses and alternative therapies started to catch my eye. Not a fan of hitting the books I often resisted, but like a petulant child who kicks and screams the entire way, I'm drawn there anyway. Over the years I studied an assortment of physical therapies and energy healing. At the same time I explored the world of Spirit and our connection to it. This was a whole new world and I was like a kid in a candy store. Not only did I speak with my old friend, but at times it appeared there were others. Often I would sense a group or some type of panel giving counsel and encouragement. I was happy here. Coming to understand that I exist far beyond the physical and connecting to that part of me that was connected to everything.

Life looks very different from this perspective. It creates a balance between the often chaotic pace and challenges of life and the magical mix of expansion and calm that connecting to Spirit brings.

So I spent time developing this connection. In psychic circles I learned to read the energy of other people. People who had passed over connected with me and conveyed messages to give to loved ones still here. I developed a relationship with Spirit that was fun and informative. Spirit provides access to information on a completely different level. I have learned to trust that information and now use it daily in my personal life.

In 2007 no one was more surprised than me when I signed up to study NLP (Neuro Linguistic Programming).

It is the science of how we store and process information in our brain and how the language of our brain affects our lives. After attending an introduction course three times, yes three times, I filled in the form and handed it and my credit card details to the administration staff. Paying the deposit I walked to the car berating myself the entire way. What had I just done? Why had I just done it? What on earth was I doing taking on study involving the mind? I was working with Spirit. It made no sense to me at all and I was angry with myself, I was fuming!

All I wanted to do was turn around and go back inside, say it was a mistake and get them to please withdraw my enrolment. Something prevented me from doing that, so I left.

Approximately one month later as I sat in class mentally stewing over the benefits of this course and why I was there, a large transparent piece of the jigsaw puzzle floated down from above and hovered directly out in front of me. This was another way that Spirit chose to pass on information. I would sometimes see transparencies of objects, scenes or words for a short time. This time it was a puzzle piece. The class was in full swing and the facilitator was speaking but I tuned out and focused on the jigsaw piece. It rotated slowly and then stopped with a slight clunk, as though it had found its exact spot and completed the picture. In that moment as I looked at it the reason I was in the room became very clear. This 'mind' study had been a missing piece of my own picture. With it I would have the ability to assist people on all levels, body, mind and Spirit.

As this realisation sank in I felt all resistance to the course dissolve and the puzzle piece faded and then was gone. You probably guessed it, the course was actually fantastic. It appears that this is just another example of Spirit dragging me kicking and screaming to something that was hugely beneficial for me personally and would also enhance my work with others.

I now know that I have been watched over by Spirit. The benefits of developing a closer relationship with it are enormous. Whether I am giving advice, get shown images or simply feel its presence, I know it is always there. Like a trusted advisor or support network, Spirit is ready to offer assistance and guidance at a moment's notice. I have spent years learning to recognise, accept and act on this guidance.

Wanting only the best for you it presents circumstances and nudges you towards your purpose. My experience has been that any resistance is met with patience, persistence and love.

Ultimately remembering that each and of every one of us is a unique expression of Spirit is liberating. This frees you to get on with your life, the life that only you can lead. There is nothing more fulfilling than acknowledging this, accepting it and stepping out to be whom you are here to be.

Those original words spoken over 15 years ago now make perfect sense. These days a connection to Spirit is woven into my life each and every day. I access its support and wisdom for myself and in the healing work I do for clients. Importantly, learning to make that connection is not something I did just for me. Others can be taught to do this for themselves. With a work history as a facilitator it is a perfect fit. Teach people to make their own connection with Spirit. From there they can access support and guidance and recognise their own power and potential to create their lives.

I get it now. Amazing that one little comment can unfold in my life in such a way. My relationship with Spirit, as with all relationships, continues to evolve and grow. It seems so natural, yet remarkable at the same time. These days when I'm given advice I no longer wonder,

"Who said that?"

I listen, I smile and I say, "Thank you old friend."

Personal Notes

CHAPTER 16

The Angel

By Steve Coleman

Set this down: Go quietly into the natural world and talk with me. I am the Angel of Love, Truth, Beauty and Care in the world.

In me you will find guidance to your life's mission. We are of an order ancient yet timeless, for we do not dwell in the time and space of humans, our Angelic world comes into existence when it is needed, it is always there, however not always manifesting. Questions are our beacon light, asking questions we know that we are needed, and that we can help should you just stop, be still and listen to us with your being. Go now and write to those who like to ask questions and walk in open spaces, high place where the trees and wind of ever changing life blow. "Go now."

Tomorrow you will see an Angel.

Wow! I thought. That will be exciting, where will it happen? What will 'it' be like? Will it know me? What will I have to do?

As we sat, all 20 of us, in our twice-guided, daily reflection, those questions cascaded into my now not-so relaxed meditative mind. "An Angel!" "Wow!"

We were several days into a beginners' retreat at the Findhorn community just outside of Forres in the north-east of Scotland near Inverness (yes, Loch Ness country).

The year; 1979, and the beginning of the northern winter. The snow drifts had already prevented my partner and me from venturing further on our Brit Rail pass to John O'Groat's – the 'Top'.

The Findhorn community, which began humbly some years earlier at the Findhorn Caravan Park a few kilometres away, was now firmly established, with its official public interface in the old and previously neglected hotel at Cluny Hill.

There was still much serious renovation happening, this was a quite practical, yet critical thread in the evolution of the new Centre, destined to become a nexus of planetary healing and stewardship and, as we now know, a global centre of spirituality, ecology and holistic learning all in one.

You can check out the Findhorn Community at https://www.findhorn.org

The first days at Findhorn were spent attending workshops on attunement with our inner selves, with others, and with the unseen elements of the natural world, Elementals, Devas, Angels and the overriding universal source of all that is.

For a 28-eight-year-old who had grown up on an island off North Queensland, Australia, with little experience of international travel other than a trip or two across the Tasman Sea to New Zealand. Coping with the jetlag and the overwhelming hubbub of the London 'big smoke' was quite enough let alone accommodating notions of Faeries, Nature Spirits and Angels.

Still, I was curious and somehow knew that this was exactly right for me at the time.

That Angel did appear, yet neither at the place nor in the context that I tried to imagine.

Being the diligent student that I was, listening to every utterance of the current speaker, following every instruction, and I have to say, pushing the boundaries, I quickly and easily slipped into the mental and physical gear of attunement.

Simply put, attunement, I discovered, was the sensation of being aware of things happening around me and not thinking at all about any part of it, rather than intellectualising perceived connections. I also realised the attunement was a relabelling of what I had already experienced as a child, playing in the bush outside our simple bush house on that North Queensland island. To play effectively and to play productively as I always did, I had to be switched into the 'toys'... the trees, the rocks and the running water in the creek at the back, the soil and the leaf litter of the vine scrubs, and of course, the abundant array of creepy crawlies that lived amongst it all, the latter pouring great significance of being switched in for personal safety reasons.

Recreating this kind of nonphysical space in a foreign country in the company of other humans was a totally different ball game.

It seemed most people in my life so far were switched in to people and didn't understand the bush stuff. Not to worry.

Our beautiful, gifted and totally understanding group facilitator had it covered.

Attuning with other human beings was simple. Sit or stand in a circle, hands lightly joined, respond to the leader's gentle prompts and relax in a state of passive alertness.

This was simple attunement with other human beings, and with practice it became for me, a constructive, subtle and very powerful tool to connect with others on a nonphysical reality. Did I try it with nonhumans at Cluny Hill? Yes, and I probably pushed the boundaries a little further than I should have.

In the course of boundary-pushing however, I was granted consistent opportunity to receive sensations from that with which I attuned. These mental sensations filtered through as key words and eventually as coherent sentences… no visuals… until the twice daily reflection on the 'Angel tomorrow' day.

Attuned now, sitting with hands lightly joined sitting in a circle of beautiful refurbished chairs in the Cluny Sanctuary, the energy flowed.

I 'saw' in my minds-eye two fuzzy clouds of white light (my partner and me) facing each other, although there were no tell-tale physical features apparent. The two 'us' clouds that merged yet maintained their separate identities, then intertwined into a single upward spiralling column of white, shining cloud. The column still spiralling upwards spread out at the top and began to take a form with projections horizontally to the sides and a smaller and further 'blob' emerging from the top.

The 'Angel promise' from the day before seeped into the vista too, it came along with that 'other' part of me now, witness to that extraordinary, totally new and totally beautiful phenomenon. That exact same instant it seemed the spiral column, the whiteness, the projections, became one, a single entity complete with body, head, and 'wings'. It was a manifestation on an energy level of our union as partners on planet earth. It was a projection of our twofold collective spirit, and it turns out, our life time and our overarching guide, benefactor and at times our troubleshooting mentor.

From that moment on I knew an older version of me was left behind forever. All was now a new playing field where the energy world of people and invisible 'entities' were real and alive. The possibilities I could see as a result of this epiphany seemed endless.

Attunement was the way to go from here on… and it has been to the moment of writing these very words. With more investigation, practice and reflection, it has become the norm in my life to the point of being on call 24/7.

The journey since the 'Angel of tomorrow' day has been a humbling experience. There is so much power on that 'new' energy playing field.

Did I ever see the Angel again?

Yes… whenever a reminder was needed on where I ought to be, what I needed to do and when I needed to do it. All I had to do was go to that place in my mind's eye. The Angel would be there as it is right now, and will forever be.

The Angel is our relationship, its presence infused with the subliminal power and timeless qualities of our planet earth, solar system and we-inspiring cosmos.

It is also the third person (who knows extra stuff) of our relationship or, should you prefer a pedantic version, a synergistic completion of two combined energies.

To share the company of these two dazzlingly beautiful, wise and liberated energies as travelling companions is indeed a gift and I am eternally grateful. Should you be prompted for further enquiry, here is a short excerpt from Dorothy MacLean's 1980 publication

To Hear the Angels Sing. It is from a chapter on Humans and Angels and presents a picture wider than the scope of the personal experience described above.

Angels. Then, show us our future, though they would not use that term. To them the future is contained within the present. Though we do not always perceive it, we are whole beings now, and must accept what we are. However as the Angels have not come by our human path, they cannot serve as a sign post labelled, 'This is the way for we have trodden it.' But the planet has many way showers. Many great teachers religious or otherwise have walked the earth, and from each one we can learn. Yet the Angels from their vantage point and from the interplay and our consciousness can see what we truly are, can see the steps in front of us, and can help us connect to our divine origin and goal. Now we can consciously seek their cooperation.

© Steve Coleman

Personal Notes

CHAPTER 17

Angels and Auras

By Selina Seah

1. When did I first become aware of them?

2. What did they look or sound like?

3. When did I first work with them?

4. What was their greatest help or other great experience?

5. Do I teach others how to connect and work with them?

Since I was a young child, say four or five years old, I've been sensitive to certain places. I remember telling my parents I didn't want to go to sleep because there was an old lady near my bed. My parents told me I was making up stories and that I should just 'go to sleep'. It was when I was 11 years old that I had a very defining moment which made me very aware that there are many things invisible to the human eyes, yet coexist with us humans.

I was also 11 years old when my family shifted to a new home, a beautiful apartment called 'The Vermillion'. It was a brand new apartment and I remember very clearly how mum and dad would take us there to visit whilst they cleaned up the place. (That was before we shifted in properly.) Our beds had not been delivered yet and I would lie on a mattress on the floor and stare out the window, looking at the sky.

What happened very vividly one afternoon, was when I was gazing at the clouds in the sky… all of a sudden, I realised that there was a very beautiful lady, like a Fairy, with beautiful hair ornaments and a long flowing gown standing right there in the middle of the clouds and looking directly at me!

At first I thought I was dreaming or imagining – I blinked my eyes yet she was still there. She was so beautiful, so graceful and she was a clear as a picture standing amongst the clouds.

I tried to call out to my parents to ask them to come and see this beautiful Fairy/Goddess… I don't really know who or what she was. Surprisingly no one heard me and I continued to 'admire' that phenomenon in the sky.

Then suddenly the clouds started to move and I remember my heart was beating with so much excitement when I saw different animals appearing in the sky. It was like a whole new world hidden behind the clouds: oh my God there really is a heaven and there are people and animals living in there too!

I cannot remember how long that vision lasted, but as usual, by the time my parents came in to look for me… they saw nothing except for clouds and the blue sky. I described to my parents exactly how the beautiful lady looked with her hair ornaments and her lovely gown. I even drew a picture to show them, only to be told that I should have been reading a book instead of wasting my time day dreaming!

But something very special happened that day, and my parents stopped telling me that I was 'day dreaming'.

That night, my aunty invited us to a plant nursery. We were walking and admiring the greenery and right in front of us was a sculpture of an ancient Chinese Goddess. I could not believe my eyes; the sculpture looked exactly like the 'lady' I had seen in the sky. Same hair ornaments, same dress!

I showed my parents the drawing of the vision again and clearly, it was exactly how the sculpture of the Chinese goddess looked. How could I have drawn the exact details of a sculpture I had never seen before?

It was a very special day for me, I was unable to explain or understand what I had seen, but deep down… I knew that there is definitely a divine presence in my life.

As I grew up and reached adulthood, I have come to realise that I have been divinely blessed and protected in many ways.

One distinct encounter of divine protection was when I was 18 years old. I was a student in a music college; I was also giving piano lessons to children in a local music school. That afternoon I had to rush off to teach the children, and a kind schoolmate offered to give me a ride there on her red scooter.

We were riding along happily when my friend realised that her brakes were not working. The traffic light ahead turned red and all the cars were slowing to a halt… except that our scooter would not slow down and we were heading for a crash with the car in front of us.

I was very scared, and I remember my friend trying her best to press on the brake handles, but to no avail.

I kept saying, *"Oh God oh God, we're going to crash! What do we do?"*

I wasn't particularly very religious at that age, but it's funny how instinctively that you somehow begin to pray when you think you are going to die!

My mum used to chant a Buddhist mantra, *"Om Mani Padme Hum"* when she prayed, and during that time I had no idea what it meant. But I began repeating the chant whilst preparing for the 'crash'.

What happened next I really do not know.

All I know was I ended up standing on the road with my helmet and I saw my friend lying there with the scooter beside her. Some parts from the wheels started falling out and I started to chase after a piece.

All the vehicles were in stationary mode as the lights were still on red; I went back to help my friend and pull the scooter to the side of the road before the lights turned green again.

Thankfully my friend was not badly injured; she had bruises and some minor cuts on her knees and calves.

What I could not explain was the fact that I had not sustained a single scratch, no bleeding, nothing! To this day I have wondered how I had managed to jump of a moving scooter without being hurt and how did I end up standing there?

There must have been divine intervention that saved both my friend and I. In case you are wondering, yes the bike crashed, into a white Mercedes that was in front of us, but no one was badly injured.

Today I have come to accept my gift of intuition and connection with the Angels, guide and ascended Masters. Every day it's a miracle to see how they guide us humans through signs, dreams, vision and messages.

To me, nothing in life is coincidence. So just when you think you only 'just had a coincidence', you may want to take a breath and smile… that coincidence could have been a visit from an Angel, giving you divine guidance and messages!

About Auras, what do I know?

As Albert Einstein explained, "Everything is Energy." Like music, energy has its vibrations and its different levels of frequency. Human beings are also 'energy'. Our forefathers have known about this important fact since ancient times. They call it the AURA, the energy field that surrounds us and CHAKRAS the energy centre with us.

Aura and chakras are not new discoveries.

Teaching people the benefits of understanding that we are all 'Energy', using auras and chakras is something very important to me. Our unique energy blueprint contains life-changing information that can help attract more happiness, abundance and success into our lives.

My clients know me as the Energy Alchemist because I can read a person's aura and chakras and help them determine areas where they are suffering from energy deficiencies and blockages that are leading them to feel disconnected from themselves. Once we understand our energy blueprint and know what our inner blockages are, it becomes easier to overcome emotional blocks and keep ourselves in alignment, regaining control and mastery of our lives. While I have the gift of intuition, but to see is to believe. I am glad and feel blessed to be able to validate my readings with technology which has helped my clients understand their invisible aura and chakras.

Science has now given us an opportunity to see our energy.

Together with Vincent Oh, my dearest husband and business partner, I founded "The Aura Chakra Company" – a one-stop place for people to come for no invasive aura scanning. Within seconds clients get to see their very own aura energy and their chakra systems. Their energy empowerment journey begins and we have many 'soul'utions for our clients wanting to optimise their energies and live a 'chakra-charged' life, be it our products, coaching or therapies.

To date I have done more than 30,000 readings worldwide and continue to teach and speak about the infinite potential of our energies – our 'invisible power'.

Some people refer to the aura as a halo surrounding an individual, maybe something like an invisible cloud. Auras are simply the energy fields that surround a person. This energy field – the aura – unfolds in different colours and these colours are not cast in stone, they can change.

Our aura can be affected by various external interactive elements. Many people cannot see their aura or the auras of others but there is often an intuitive feeling that can give you an idea of a person's general aura.

For example, when you meet someone for the first time, why is it that for some individuals you will find an instant connection and rapport, whereas there will be others that you can't wait to find the exit door?

Some will call it a vibe or a gut feeling, but what's really happening is that you are picking up the energy of the other party's aura.

A simple example would be – a happy person. His or her aura will be bright and welcoming, which is usually clearly seen in their behaviour, interaction and even their choice of colours!

Every colour that is found in an aura depicts a different meaning. We are all our own rainbows vibrating as energy and our aura is simply our energy blueprint.

The colours in our auras are determined by our personal strengths, health, awareness and our quality of life.

Your unique aura is the gateway to a very powerful self-discovery journey. We do not attract what we want, but rather what we are. Your energy speaks even before you do. When we start to identify and understand our auras, we begin a new journey of understanding our emotions and inner motivations. This deeper understanding of ourselves will help us to master our strong qualities and at the same time become aware of our weaknesses.

By understanding that everyone has their own unique energy and colour vibrations, we begin to go beyond skin deep and just your personality. We will embrace the beauty of different colours with acceptance and mastery.

What your Aura colours say about YOU! (Taken from *The Invisible Power* book)

1. **RED** – Reds are practical people who desire to achieve success and results. They are curious, insistent and passionate about living their lives to the fullest. Many sportsmen, leaders and good sales people carry a red aura.

2. **ORANGE** – Orange personalities are natural born leaders who bring with them creativity and motivation. Being in control of their realities is important to them. Many business owners, architects and developers carry an orange aura.

3. **YELLOW** – Yellows are bright, creative and fun people. They are intelligent and charismatic people who enjoy a good social network. Yellows make ideal team members and have good initiative. Many students, celebrities and freelancers carry a yellow aura.

4. **GREEN** – Green personalities are natural communicators who enjoy being with their families. Security and growth are important to greens. Many teachers, secretaries and social workers carry a green aura.

5. **BLUE** – Blues are very caring and loyal people. Peace and contentment is what they seek. Blues are always there for a friend in need. Many doctors, counsellors and healers carry a blue aura.

6. **INDIGO** – Indigos have deep feelings and perceptions of life. They have strong inner values and belief systems. Truth and trust are all very important to them. Many musicians, artists and writers carry an indigo aura.

7. **VIOLET** – Violets possess strong knowledge and intuition. They have emotional depth and carry a magnetic radiance. Realising their visions and honing their creativity is very important for the violets. You can find violets in politicians, authors and CEOs.

8. **WHITE** – Intelligent and careful. Whites enjoy having their personal space. Whites are quiet and sensitive individuals who function on an intuitive and spiritual platform rather than an 'over analytical' basis. You can find whites in spiritual teachers, healers and surgeons.

Selena

Personal Notes

CHAPTER 18

By Wanda Shipton

I still have vivid memories of being in a green cot in the attic, which was my bedroom in my family's home in England. While I was in my cot, up until the age of two, I experienced my body floating upwards each night in a beautiful golden light and being rocked from head to toe while listening to high-pitch sounds and feeling relaxed and loved. I could feel the sound of the golden light on my body as I fell into a deep sleep. I thought everyone experienced this when going to sleep. There were light vibrations at my head and feet. Looking back now I realise they must have been Angels. At the time I didn't see their faces, all I knew was they would not harm me; they were my friends. I could also hear and feel these sounds throughout the day if I sat in a particular place in the attic, feeling these sounds going through my body made me feel peaceful and happy. I remember seeing what I called moon men; they were golden orbs that appeared at my window. Mum's explanation was – I had a good imagination.

My mum said I always had pencils in my hand and that I had been drawing from the age of two years old. My father sketched portraits and he encouraged me to also develop these skills. I have been drawing people's faces in shade from an early age not knowing who there were or why I had drawn them. People would ask who they were; I knew I just needed to draw them. It wasn't that I was compelled to draw them rather that I have something to express that needed to come out. I realised this was a form of channelling. At school we did pastel drawings and I loved it as it was quick and spontaneous. The teacher said that I was able to draw better that her, and she asked me to show the other pupils how to shade and use colour. I didn't have to think about it, I just knew what to do and the Angels helped me to do this. This was the start of recognising my gifts and communication with the Angels. I painted purple shadows and many colours on still-life artwork. Helping my school friends allowed me to experience and experiment with a range of colours and how they related to each other.

Later I started painting with oil paints and I would get messages from Spirit to change one part of my paintings, this would alter the complete picture. I trusted their guidance and eventually my paintings were exhibited in art shows. I was aware that my pastel drawings of faces were that of my guides and of other peoples' guides. Then I started to do Psychic drawings and readings for others at a professional level. I went on to learn counselling and achieved a Degree in Psychology.

Angels visited me in dreams; on the astral plane, and during meditation. Sometimes I saw them as orbs in many different colours. One red orb vibrated so strongly at the end of my bed, that I knew it must have a message for me. The next day I happened to look in a book and saw that the Goddess Quan Yin appeared as a red orb. I painted her and she became one of my guides. I would paint different ascended masters, like Saint Germain, Melchizedeck, Isis, Sai Baba, even Jesus and Mary and many more who connected with me. It seemed that painting them enabled me to channel them. I have seen many ghosts and spirits, those who have passed on and I found myself talking to them and helping them to pass over peacefully. Some souls would not go on and would hang around; my Angels would then help me to send them on. After meditating one night, I went to bed and a young child, about six years old, visited me. Her hair was blonde and messy, she looked like she hadn't been very well looked after, she had a tube coming out of her left nostril, and I recognised it as medical apparatus for breathing. I looked at her for a long time and even asked her who she was and why she had come to see me, however, her gaze was fixed on a shiny silver object that was illuminated by the moon rays through the window. I could only see the top part of her as her bottom half faded through the bed. Intuitively I knew she had died in hospital and was ready to move on.

My guides took me to other planes to help those trapped by their own guilt and fear. They also took me to other places in space and time – back to past lives and future events, even to different star systems – places of coloured crystal lights where the beings were so loving and caring.

These light beings were tall and slender, humanoid in appearance with light for hair. Some had wing like energy around them. Again I painted many celestial Angels and Pleiadean light beings. Then I was introduced to the Sirian beings from the Orion constellation that guided me with scientific information. They were tall with light-blue coloured auras. They connected with my ancient Egyptian past lives.

When I draw a person's guide it would start with a burst of colours. I would not know whether it was male or female, young or old. Out of the swirling colours I could see a face emerging, and brought out their features. There were also symbols and animal spirits. Where the symbols were placed on the painting meant something different. It could relate to the conscious or unconscious, past or present, grounded or restricted. I was shown the person's past lives and given messages from Spirit as well as their name. The Guides do not actually move my hand; they guide me through my intuition. So when I draw with pastel or paint I feel intuitively where to go and what to do. I don't always see the guide then paint them. I may see a number of the spirits around when I first meet the person then I allow the guide that is meant to be drawn at the time; through intuition rather than image. It could be an Ascended Master, Angel, Guide, Native, Goddess or Light Being.

The first Guide I drew was a Native American Guide called Silver Eagle. You can see my painting of Silver Eagle on my native Medicine drum. I could feel him behind me, when I painted this, however, I did not have a lot to do with Native Americans at the time and it was not until I painted him that it gave me the confirmation. Silver Eagle encouraged me to learn about the native tribes and their spirituality and to set up my own Indian Tipi in the grounds of my Healing Centre that I ran on the Sunshine Coast. There were ceremonies conducted by the native Lakota tribe that came from America to initiate and bless the Medicine Wheel that they had created for me – they introduced me to animal spirits like the snake and the owl.

Meditation helped me to open my third-eye more fully. I believe it is the key to enlightenment, evolution and ascension. So I started meditation classes and created meditation CDs to help people on their journey. Often I would be talking to a group of people in a workshop and I would find myself saying things that I never knew about. Later I was aware I had channelled this information while astral travelling. One of my memories of being in a different dimension was choosing to move through a double brick wall, going backward and forward to feel what it was like. I could not feel anything really, only waves of air. However, I have felt touches from people that I have met while astral travelling. I know I have been healed and have healed others on that dimension. Another memory is where I merged with my Guide, and as I was coming back into my body we separated and he gave me four pages which I read and understood, but when I came back into my body I could not remember anything and felt that I had failed. He assured me that I would remember at the right time, which I did. The four pages were four workshops that I successfully facilitated.

My Ascended Masters taught me the process of Ascension, helping me to witness my astral body coming back into my physical body; what it is like when we die – life after death – what happens to us after we leave this plane. When

I left my physical body I had the sensation of rising. Then I began to fly over the land through the sky and stars. It felt the same as it does here on the physical plane. I could hear, see, feel and think. I had the will to move and made decisions, this was not like a dream where you sit back and watch what happens. This is who I am after I die physically; if I didn't go back to my body. Sometimes I would teach people how to levitate on the astral, and showed them that by kicking up their feet, they could lift off. My Guides also sent me to many places of beauty, colour & love on the astral level.

A hypnotherapist taped a session with me where I travelled to other star systems. One of which was the Pleiades constellation. It was there that I looked after star children. One of the most beautiful experiences was when I felt an alien light being inside me pointing a very long slender finger. After the session the hypnotherapist said he also saw a graceful benevolent light being pointing her index finger. These experiences have helped me to channel draw these beings of light for myself and others. Through their connection I have learned about strands of DNA, and frequencies that affect and heal the brain creating new energy links towards evolution. All my experiences with Guides, Masters, Angels and Light Beings, energy, sound frequencies and colours are shared in the spirit guide drawings and art workshops.

I have learned that when we are born all our senses are one, colour and sound are one. We can hear the colour and see the vibration, as it was when I was a baby. I am here to help people to become more empowered and to love themselves.

Blessings, Wanda Shipton

About the Contributors

Dr Linet Amalie

Dr Linet Amalie PhD was born hearing impaired; she is a natural psychic medium, a professional member of the IPA and has been working professionally in the health, healing and psychic industry for over 30 years.

Her lifetime goal is to raise the consciousness of humanity in relation to (personal) spiritual development which will then empower the individual to heal themselves and others from within; she is also a professional listener to the Industry offering professional debriefing, counselling and supervision.

Linet is also a qualified Mental Health Practitioner and the founder and owner of "The Healing Centre TM."

She is an Accredited Education Provider and Certified Member of IICT, has created successful multiple online education courses including counselling courses, meditation & mindfulness training, audio books and CD's.

She can be contacted via her paging service on 0400 083 093, and her website which is www.drlinet.com

Julia Anais

Since discovering meditation as a daily practice with powerful "I am" music by Dr Wayne Dyer, Julia found a connection to her inner wisdom which has brought peace and harmony to her being and a less stressful way to live.

Julia feels a strong passion to share the source of this inner peace and believes opening up to Mindfulness is something many can benefit from.

Julia's hope is to practice; through Mindfulness, to help others open up and be in touch with themselves and allow the healing connection that will create a balanced and harmonious way of being.

Email: littlemindfulness@outlook.com
https://fb.me/littlemindfulnes

Sonia Crystella

Sonia has spent more than 40 years living and practicing the holistic and spiritual path. After a NDE as a young teenager, Sonia's life changed, she searched for a way to heal her sick body through diet, and the mind body soul connection. She is now an Anti-ageing DNA researcher, energy clearer and public speaker.

With a published book

"Unlocking the Secrets to Longevity"

Sonia understands the science and metaphysics of ageing and disease; she believes oxygen, diet and meditation are the tools that help us stay young, along with energy and the impact it has on our day to day life. She frequently works with the energetic frequencies to support balanced environments and buildings. She is a member of *The Australian Epigenetic Alliance* AEpiA

Email: info@soniacrystella.com
www.soniacrystella.com

Leila Dal-Zotto

Leila has guided many individuals, families and businesses over the last 25 years to have more clarity and direction. Throughout her own life Leila has experienced amazing spiritual phenomena that have let her know her role in this life. When it comes to being a spiritual medium Leila allows whatever is to take place in a session to happen. It could be speaking to loved ones who have passed over, or giving clarity and direction in your life or spiritual healing. It is the channelling of divine guidance through that is truly inspirational and healing.

Email: leilasconnections@hotmail.com

Karen Wilson

Karen Wilson is an author, speaker, facilitator and intuitive healer. Combining Science and Spirituality Karen offers courses in transformation and tailors personal sessions for clients to achieve optimal results. Karen's passion is to empower others make inspired change and live an authentic life that they love. The author of the book *Change Made Easy*.

Karen lives in Central Victoria, Australia. For more details and to contact Karen visit

www.Changingwillows.com

Steve Coleman

Steve is an author, educator, father and outdoorsman. He has worked with a wide variety of companies, schools and organisations including several QLD high schools, most of the private secondary schools in Townsville and Hinterland, local sports clubs and Youth Services of QLD, Army cadet units and Queensland Guides and Scouts.

His professional associations include the International Yoga Teachers Association, Queensland College of Teachers, Queensland Writers' Centre. Townsville Writers and Publishers, and Queensland Outdoor Recreation Federation. He is also a Registered Consultant with Kolbe Corporation in Phoenix Arizona USA.

Steve has lived, travelled and worked throughout New Zealand, Papua New Guinea, USA, Canada, Singapore, UK, Malaysia, Cook Islands.

He is the Author of "Decisions, Decisions!" and 4 children's books. Steve lives in Queensland Australia

For more information on Steve; please go to

www.howtomaketherightdesisionseverytime.com
www.greentalepublishing.com.au

Wanda Shipton

Wanda Shipton has worked in the Metaphysical arena for a number of years - healer and teacher, with a degree in Psychology and Diploma in Hypnotherapy. As an artist Wanda has exhibited her art in many different mediums and subjects. Combining her gifts of clairvoyance and painting allowed her to connect with people, bringing forward their Spirit Guides and Angels through her creative channels of Intuition and art. Today Wanda conducts one on one sessions drawing Angels with a Psychic Reading. She also facilitates Guide Drawing Workshops where she guides others to learn how to channel art to draw their own Guides.

Email: wandashipton@yahoo.com.au
www.wandasangelart.com

Selina Seah

Selena's clients know her as the Energy Alchemist because of her ability to read a person's aura and chakras, which helps them determine areas where they are suffering from energy deficiencies and blockages that are leading them to feel disconnected from themselves.

Together with Vincent Oh; her husband and business partner, she founded "The Aura Chakra Company" – a one stop place for people to come for no invasive aura scanning.

Books:

1. The Invisible Power- The 9 Laws of Highly Successful People

2. The Success DNA of Extraordinary Entrepreneurs – How to go from invisible to invincible in your business

www.thechakracompany.com
www.selinaseah.com

Personal Notes

Final Word

Dear Reader,

In summing up; be focused on quality breathing. Raise your energy levels by the power of your amazing breath – meditation and affirmations; and redirect your thoughts from negative to positive.

Work with your Angels and Guides by trusting God, your intuition and your sensory abilities. Expect no less than the best you can achieve; by doing your best.

Create your own happiness and share your knowledge and talents with others.

I do hope that some of what works for me will also work for you.

IF I CAN DO IT, ANYONE CAN!

Lovingly Yours,

Kawena

About the Author

Kawena (Gwen Gordon) is now 89 years young and a second time author showing you are never too old to live your dreams.

Born in NSW, Australia, in 1928, Kawena lived what may be called a normal life as wife and mother. It was always her dream as a little girl to sing and at the same time she had a fascination in the power of the mind.

At 30 years of age the family moved to the Gold Coast in Queensland. Once the family grew up and moved out, Kawena learnt to sing at 45 years of age. Here she discovered the power of the breath and her whole life turned around being much more energised, motivated and confident than she had ever been.

Out went the old Gwen Gordon and in came Kawena.

Kawena spent the next 22 years singing up and down the Gold Coast with the Labrador Senior Citizens Group.

Kawena also took her own singing group to nursing homes and other senior citizen venues.

Having experienced such joy and happiness in singing and understanding the importance of the breath, Kawena wanted to learn more about the power of quality breath.

Kawena constantly explored and studied the mind, the breath, meditation and different healing modalities such as sound and colour vibration, reiki and crystal healing and realised quality breathing was the key ingredient for high energy, happiness and motivation.

Kawena then moved from singing to teaching meditation and motivation in her regular meditation group plus High Energy Motivation workshops for the next 20 years.

Kawena enjoys the enthusiasm of the younger generation who are looking for purpose and direction, are keen to understand and improve their life, find their own happiness and have more energy. At the same time, teaching the 30–50-year-old unemployed to be happy and motivated was immensely rewarding.

As Kawena followed her dreams, she now wants to share her story and motivate others to be happy and confident to follow their dreams.

Living on the beautiful Gold Coast in Queensland, Kawena's greatest joy in life is helping people understand what wonderful potential lives in each and every one of us and it doesn't matter how old or how young you are, you can always achieve your dream with the power of quality breathing and the power of the mind.

RECOMMENDED RESOURCES

Recommended Resources

For more inspiration and motivation visit:

www.ExpandingEnergies.com.au

- **Kawena's Book:**

  "Happiness is Just A Breath Away"

- **Kawena's Personal Guidance and Mentoring Cards**

Guided CDs, Sessions, Workshops by Kawena

- **The Art of Breathing Made Easy CD**

  Quality breathing helps supply the body with more oxygen which helps us to achieve a much better quality of life, and our health will improve dramatically, especially in the immune system.

- **Meditation Made Easy CD**

  Meditation can help in all areas of your life, from reducing stress and tension, to becoming more creative and more aware. My meditations are designed for both beginners and advanced.

- **Meditation Made Easy For Children CD**

  Suitable for three years upwards; in the style of storytelling so children can learn to visualise and use their imagination.

- **Private Session** – Life Direction

Angel card readings

- **Private Mentoring and Motivation Session**
- **Workshops:** Happiness High Energy and Motivation

www.ingramcontent.com/pod-product-compliance
Lightning Source LLC
Chambersburg PA
CBHW060019100426
42740CB00010B/1532

* 9 7 8 1 9 2 5 2 8 8 7 6 6 *